THE ULTIMATE GUIDE

2023
TRAEGER GRILL
& SMOKER

COOKBOOK FOR BEGINNERS

1000 DAYS OF IRRESISTIBLE BBQ RECIPES:

Master the Craft of Grilling, Smoking, and Delight Your Taste Buds

Epicurean Thomas

TABLE OF CONTENT

INTRODUCTION

Welcome to the Traeger Grill Master's Cookbook, your ultimate guide to unlocking the full potential of your Traeger grill and mastering the art of outdoor cooking. Whether you're an experienced pitmaster or a beginner in the world of grilling, this comprehensive cookbook will lead you on a flavorful adventure, introducing you to various recipes, techniques, and tips for elevating your backyard culinary experiences.

Traeger grills, like the Traeger, are well-known for their versatility and the distinct smoky flavors they impart to dishes through the use of all-natural hardwood pellets. From searing steaks and slow-smoking ribs to roasting vegetables and baking mouthwatering desserts, the Traeger Grill Master's Cookbook presents a diverse collection of recipes that showcase the boundless potential of Traeger cooking.

In this cookbook, we move beyond traditional grilling concepts to delve into the art of infusing your dishes with layers of flavor, using a wide range of ingredients and innovative techniques. From classic barbecue favorites to inventive twists on international cuisine, each recipe has been meticulously crafted to accentuate the extraordinary versatility and capabilities of your Traeger grill.

The Traeger Grill Master's Cookbook is more than just a compilation of recipes. It's a vast resource that empowers you with the knowledge and skills needed to become a true maestro of Traeger cooking. Throughout the pages of this cookbook, you'll encounter priceless tips, tricks, and techniques aimed at helping you perfect your grilling game, from temperature control and smoke infusion to maintaining and cleaning your Traeger grill.

At the core of the Traeger Grill Master's Cookbook is the belief that preparing and sharing meals with loved ones is a communal experience, fostering connections, creating cherished memories, and bringing joy to both the cook and the diners. We invite you to embrace the essence of community, gather your family and friends, and embark on a gastronomic journey of exploration.

Whether you're hosting a backyard barbecue, tailgating with your buddies, or enjoying a meal with your family, the Traeger Grill Master's Cookbook will be your reliable companion, offering inspiration, guidance, and delectable recipes to make each grilling event truly unforgettable.

So fire up your Traeger grill, let the aromatic smoke envelop your senses, and let the Traeger Grill Master's Cookbook be your trusted guide on this culinary expedition. Get ready to create exceptional meals, revel in the joy of outdoor cooking, and become a true master of the art of grilling with the Traeger Grill Master's Cookbook.

CHAPTER 1

WELCOME TO THE TRAEGER GRILL MASTER'S COOKBOOK

EXPLORING THE CULINARY REALM OF TRAEGER GRILLS

The Legacy of Traeger Grills

Embarking on a journey that spans decades, Traeger Grills has established a rich and captivating history. It all began in the 1980s when Joe Traeger, a visionary hailing from Mount Angel, Oregon, embarked on a mission to revolutionize outdoor cooking. Inspired by the delectable flavors and tenderness achieved through slow-cooking meat over open wood fires, Joe sought to recreate that remarkable wood-fired taste and make it accessible to all.

In 1985, Joe Traeger achieved a groundbreaking milestone by patenting the first pellet grill. This ingenious invention would forever transform the landscape of outdoor cooking. Unlike traditional charcoal or gas grills, pellet grills harnessed the power of all-natural hardwood pellets as their primary fuel source. These pellets, meticulously crafted from compressed hardwood, provided a controlled and consistent burn, generating a steady supply of heat and smoke.

Through his innovative design, Joe Traeger seamlessly blended modern convenience with the unparalleled flavor of wood-fired cooking. The Traeger grill swiftly captivated the hearts of outdoor enthusiasts, professional chefs, and backyard cooks alike, offering a compelling alternative to conventional grilling methods.

Over the years, Traeger Grills has remained committed to refining and elevating their products, introducing new features and technologies that enhance the grilling experience. With a relentless dedication to quality craftsmanship, Traeger utilizes durable materials and precision engineering to ensure their grills deliver exceptional performance and long-lasting durability.

As Traeger Grills continues to evolve, their passion for wood-fired cooking remains at the forefront of their innovations. With each grill meticulously crafted, they empower grill enthusiasts to unlock their culinary potential and embark on a flavorful adventure.

Today, Traeger Grills stands as a beacon of excellence in the world of outdoor cooking, inspiring grill masters to push boundaries and create extraordinary dishes that tantalize the taste buds. With a legacy built upon the fusion of tradition and innovation, Traeger Grills invites you to embark on your own wood-fired journey and discover the unparalleled joy of flavorful, perfectly cooked meals.

Pioneering Innovation and Expansion

In 2006, Traeger made a significant leap forward with the introduction of the Digital Pro Controller, a game-changing advancement in temperature control technology. This groundbreaking feature empowered users to effortlessly set and maintain precise cooking temperatures, eliminating the guesswork and ensuring consistent results with every grill session.

Driven by a commitment to meet diverse needs and preferences, the Traeger brand expanded its product line. They introduced a range of grill sizes, catering to both portable models for on-the-go grilling and larger, high-capacity grills suitable for commercial use. Recognizing the importance of versatility, Traeger also developed a wide array of accessories and add-ons, including racks, griddles, and insulation blankets, to enhance the functionality and adaptability of their grills.

Traeger Grills' unwavering dedication to innovation and a relentless pursuit of quality has made them synonymous with wood-fired cooking. Their endeavors have fostered a passionate community of Traeger enthusiasts who share a deep appreciation for the art of outdoor cooking and the extraordinary flavors that can be achieved with a Traeger grill.

Today, Traeger remains at the forefront of the industry, continuously pushing the boundaries of what's possible in wood-fired cooking.

Their extensive range of grills and smokers is meticulously designed to meet the diverse needs of backyard cooks, professional chefs, and culinary enthusiasts at every level. Whether you're searing steaks, smoking ribs, baking pizza, or roasting vegetables, Traeger grills provide a versatile platform that unleashes your culinary creativity.

The history of Traeger Grills stands as a testament to the vision and passion of Joe Traeger. His groundbreaking invention has revolutionized the way people approach outdoor cooking, bringing the art of wood-fired flavor to homes around the world. As Traeger continues to innovate and inspire, they remain at the forefront of the wood-fired cooking movement, empowering individuals to elevate their grilling game and create unforgettable culinary experiences.

Welcome to the Traeger Grill Bible Cookbook, where the rich legacy of Traeger Grills unfolds, inviting you to embark on a journey of flavor and mastery.

Variety of Traeger Grill Options

Traeger Grills takes pride in offering a diverse range of grills designed to cater to a variety of needs and preferences. Here's a breakdown of the different types of Traeger Grills available:

Pro Series:

- The Pro Series stands as Traeger's flagship line, renowned for its durability, performance, and versatility.
- These grills feature Traeger's Digital Pro Controller, enabling precise temperature control for consistent cooking results.
- Available in various sizes to accommodate different cooking capacities and spaces.
- Pro Series grills are equipped with advanced features such as WiFIRE® technology, which allows for remote control and monitoring via a smartphone app.
- Perfectly suited for both backyard grilling enthusiasts and professional chefs.

Ironwood Series:

- The Ironwood Series seamlessly combines the precision and convenience of Traeger's advanced technologies with exceptional craftsmanship.
- These grills boast the Ironwood D2 Controller, which offers WiFIRE® technology for convenient remote control and enhanced temperature accuracy.
- Ironwood grills are constructed with a double-wall stainless steel interior, ensuring superior heat retention and long-lasting durability.
- Available in various sizes, they provide ample cooking space to accommodate different needs.

Timberline Series:

- The Timberline Series represents the epitome of Traeger's grilling technology and craftsmanship.
- These premium grills deliver unmatched performance and durability, making them ideal for serious grillmasters and professionals.
- Timberline grills feature the Timberline D2 Controller, providing the most precise temperature control and advanced features like Super Smoke Mode.
- With double-wall stainless steel construction, insulated grill grates, and airtight lid gaskets, Timberline grills ensure ultimate heat retention.
- They offer the largest cooking capacity among Traeger's lineup, perfect for large gatherings and commercial use.

Tailgater Series:

- The Tailgater Series is designed for those who enjoy grilling on the go, whether it's camping, tailgating, or picnicking.
- These compact and portable grills are lightweight and easy to transport.
- Tailgater grills feature the Digital Arc Controller, allowing for precise temperature adjustments.
- Despite their small size, they offer ample cooking space to grill, smoke, and roast delicious meals wherever you go.

Ranger Series:

- The Ranger Series is Traeger's smallest and most portable option, perfect for those who want to enjoy wood-fired flavor on the road or in small spaces.
- These tabletop grills are lightweight, compact, and easy to transport.
- Ranger grills feature the Digital Arc Controller and offer versatile cooking options despite their smaller size.
- They are ideal for tailgating, camping, and apartment balconies, allowing you to enjoy the Traeger grilling experience anywhere.

Each series of Traeger Grills offers unique features and benefits, enabling you to choose the grill that best suits your cooking style, needs, and space requirements. Whether you're a backyard enthusiast, professional chef, or someone who loves grilling on the go, there's a Traeger grill designed to elevate your wood-fired cooking experience.

The versatility of Traeger grills sets them apart from traditional grilling methods, making them a versatile cooking tool for various culinary techniques. Here's an elaboration on the versatility of Traeger grills:

Grilling:

- Traeger grills excel at traditional grilling, allowing you to sear steaks, grill burgers, cook chicken, and more, imparting a perfect char and smoky flavor.
- The even heat distribution and precise temperature control of Traeger grills ensure consistent results without the need for constant flipping and monitoring.

Smoking:

- Traeger grills are renowned for their exceptional smoking capabilities, enabling you to achieve tender, juicy, and flavorful smoked meats.
- The combination of low and slow cooking with the controlled burn of all-natural hardwood pellets creates mouthwatering results, infusing the meat with rich smoky flavors.

Roasting:

- Traeger grills are perfect for roasting a variety of dishes, from whole chickens and turkeys to prime rib and pork roasts.
- The consistent temperature control and convection cooking style of Traeger grills ensure even cooking and deliciously moist results.

Baking:

- Traeger grills offer the unique ability to bake, allowing you to create wood-fired pizzas, bread, desserts, and more.
- The versatility of temperature settings and the infusion of wood-fired flavors elevate your baked goods to a new level.

Braising:

- Traeger grills are ideal for braising tough cuts of meat, such as brisket or short ribs, which require low and slow cooking in a moist environment.
- The combination of the grill's controlled heat and the addition of liquid in the cooking process creates tender and succulent results.

Barbecuing:

- Traeger grills are perfect for authentic barbecue experiences, whether you're smoking ribs, slow-cooking pulled pork, or making mouthwatering brisket.
- The combination of wood-fired flavor and precise temperature control allows you to achieve the perfect texture and taste that barbecue enthusiasts crave.

The Versatility of Traeger Grills

The versatility of Traeger grills opens up a world of culinary possibilities, allowing you to explore and master various cooking techniques with ease and confidence.

Indeed, Traeger grills offer a wide range of cooking accessories that further enhance their versatility. These accessories allow you to expand your cooking options and experiment with new recipes and techniques.

Grilling racks, griddles, smoking boxes, pizza stones, and other accessories provide added functionality and flexibility to your Traeger grill, enabling you to customize your cooking experience and explore a variety of flavors.

The art of wood-fired cooking with Traeger grills combines culinary techniques with the distinctive flavors and aromas of wood smoke. Here's an elaboration on the art of wood-fired cooking with Traeger:

- Flavorful Wood Smoke: Traeger grills use all-natural hardwood pellets as fuel, infusing your dishes with rich, smoky flavors that are unmatched by other cooking methods. The choice of wood pellets, such as hickory, mesquite, apple, or cherry, allows you to experiment and create a wide range of flavor profiles to enhance your dishes.

- Temperature Control: Traeger grills provide precise temperature control, allowing you to set and maintain the desired heat level throughout the cooking process. This level of control ensures that your food is cooked to perfection, with consistent results every time.

- Low and Slow Cooking: Traeger grills excel at low and slow cooking techniques, such as smoking and braising, which are essential for achieving tender, juicy, and flavorful meats. The controlled burn of the wood pellets and the even heat distribution create a moist cooking environment that slowly breaks down collagen and renders fat, resulting in melt-in-your-mouth textures.

- Convection Cooking: Traeger grills utilize convection cooking, circulating hot air around the food, to ensure even cooking and eliminate hot spots. This technique promotes faster and more consistent cooking, allowing you to achieve perfectly cooked dishes from edge to edge.

- Versatile Cooking Surfaces: Traeger grills offer versatile cooking surfaces, including grates, racks, and inserts, to accommodate different ingredients and cooking methods. You can sear steaks over high heat, smoke ribs on low heat, and even bake pizzas or desserts with the right accessories.

- Enhancing Creativity: Wood-fired cooking with Traeger grills encourages creativity and experimentation in the kitchen. The combination of flavors from different wood pellets, seasoning blends, marinades, and rubs allows you to personalize your dishes and create unique culinary creations.

- Connecting with Tradition: Wood-fired cooking has a long-standing tradition in many cultures, evoking a sense of nostalgia and connection to culinary heritage. Using a Traeger grill not only allows you to enjoy modern convenience but also connects you to time-honored techniques and flavors of the past.

The art of wood-fired cooking with Traeger grills is a captivating and rewarding experience. It combines precise temperature control, flavorful wood smoke, and versatile cooking techniques to elevate your dishes to new levels of taste and tenderness. Whether you're grilling, smoking, roasting, baking, or braising, the art of wood-fired cooking with Traeger allows you to unleash your creativity, connect with tradition, and savor the unique flavors that only wood smoke can provide.

Mastering Your Traeger Grill

To truly master your Traeger grill and achieve exceptional cooking results, it's important to understand its key components and how to optimize their use. Here are some tips to help you make the most of your Traeger grill:

- Preheat Your Grill: Preheating your Traeger grill is essential to ensure even heat distribution and optimal cooking conditions. Allow your grill to heat up for at least 10-15 minutes before placing your food on the grates.

- Use High-Quality Wood Pellets: The type and quality of wood pellets you use can significantly impact the flavor of your food. Choose high-quality, all-natural hardwood pellets that complement the flavors you're aiming for. Experiment with different wood varieties to discover your favorite combinations.

- Clean and Maintain Your Grill: Regularly clean your grill to keep it in optimal condition. Clean the grill grates after each use to prevent buildup and ensure proper searing. Empty the ash from the fire pot regularly to maintain efficient airflow and prevent any issues with the ignition system.

- Experiment with Temperature Settings: Traeger grills offer precise temperature control, allowing you to set the desired cooking temperature. Experiment with different temperature settings to achieve the results you desire for various recipes. Adjusting the temperature can help you achieve different levels of searing, smoking, and roasting.

- Use Grill Thermometers: While Traeger grills come with built-in temperature controls, using additional grill thermometers can provide you with more accurate readings for specific cuts of meat or recipes. This allows you to monitor the internal temperature of your food and ensure it's cooked to your desired level of doneness.

- Utilize Accessories and Techniques: Take advantage of Traeger's versatile cooking accessories and techniques. Explore grilling racks, smoking boxes, and other accessories to expand your cooking options. Experiment with smoking, roasting, baking, and other techniques to explore the full potential of your Traeger grill.

- Keep an Eye on Cooking Times: Cooking times can vary based on factors like the size and thickness of the food, the cooking temperature, and the desired level of doneness. Keep an eye on the cooking progress and use recommended cooking times as guidelines, adjusting as needed to achieve your desired results.

By understanding your Traeger grill, utilizing its key components effectively, and experimenting with different techniques and flavors, you can master the art of cooking with your Traeger grill and create delicious wood-fired meals with ease. Enjoy the journey of exploring new recipes, perfecting your grilling skills, and delighting your family and friends with the flavors of Traeger.

Understanding the components

Understanding the components of your Traeger grill is essential for maximizing its performance and achieving optimal cooking results. Here's a breakdown of the key components and their functions:

- Hopper: The hopper is where you load the wood pellets that fuel your Traeger grill. It has a large capacity, allowing for extended cooking sessions without frequent refills. The hopper's design typically includes a lid for easy access and a clear window to monitor pellet levels.

- Auger: Located beneath the hopper, the auger is responsible for transferring wood pellets from the hopper to the fire pot. It operates using a motor-driven mechanism that precisely feeds the pellets into the fire pot at a controlled rate. This ensures a steady and consistent fuel supply, maintaining optimal cooking temperatures throughout the grilling process.

- Digital Controller: The digital controller serves as the command center of your Traeger grill. It allows you to set and adjust cooking temperatures with ease. The controller features a clear and user-friendly interface, providing precise temperature control for various cooking techniques such as smoking, roasting, and grilling. It may also include additional features like programmable timers and compatibility with meat probes for accurate food temperature monitoring.

- Grill Grates: The grill grates are where you place your food for grilling. They are typically made from high-quality materials such as stainless steel or cast iron. The grates offer a sturdy and reliable surface that can withstand high temperatures and provide excellent searing capabilities. Their design ensures even heat distribution, resulting in consistent cooking results across the entire grilling surface.

By understanding how these components work together, you can effectively utilize your Traeger grill and make precise adjustments to achieve your desired cooking outcomes.

Whether you're grilling, smoking, or roasting, mastering the use of these components will enhance your grilling experience and help you create delicious wood-fired meals.

The Wood-Fired Cooking System

The wood-fired cooking system of the Traeger grill is what sets it apart and creates its unique flavor profile. Here's a closer look at how the system operates and the advantages it offers:

- Wood Pellet Fuel: Wood pellets are the primary fuel source for the Traeger grill. They are available in a variety of flavors such as hickory, mesquite, apple, and cherry. These pellets are loaded into the hopper, ready to be used during the cooking process.

- Auger and Fire Pot: The auger, driven by a motor, feeds the wood pellets from the hopper into the fire pot. As the pellets enter the fire pot, they ignite and create a controlled fire. This fire generates both heat and flavorful smoke, which are key elements in wood-fired cooking.

- Flavorful Smoke Circulation: The combination of heat and smoke circulates within the cooking chamber of the grill. The smoke envelops the food, infusing it with a distinct smoky flavor. This process enhances the taste of grilled dishes and creates a signature smoky aroma that is highly sought after.

Advantages of the Wood-Fired Cooking System

- Unique Flavor Profile: The wood-fired cooking system imparts a unique and desirable flavor profile to grilled foods. The natural hardwood smoke from the pellets enhances the taste of the dishes, providing a smoky depth that cannot be replicated with other cooking methods.

- Consistent Heat Distribution: The system ensures consistent and even heat distribution throughout the cooking chamber. This allows for precise cooking, reducing the risk of overcooking or undercooking your food. The even heat distribution also eliminates hot spots, ensuring that every part of the grill surface cooks your food evenly.

- Versatility and Flavor Experimentation: The variety of available wood pellet flavors allows users to experiment with different tastes and profiles. By choosing different wood pellet flavors, grillers can tailor the flavor of their dishes to their personal preferences. This versatility adds excitement and creativity to the cooking experience.

Understanding the wood-fired cooking system empowers grillers to fully utilize the Traeger grill's capabilities. By exploring the range of available wood pellet flavors and their impact on taste, you can create a diverse array of grilled dishes, ranging from bold and smoky flavors to more subtle and nuanced profiles.

With a comprehensive understanding of your Traeger grill, including its components, functionalities, and wood-fired cooking system, you'll be well-equipped to embark on a culinary journey, confidently creating delectable dishes that showcase the unique flavors of wood-fired cooking.

Temperature Control and Management

Temperature control and management are crucial for achieving desired cooking results and maintaining consistency when grilling with your Traeger grill. Here's a breakdown of the significance of temperature control and practical tips for managing temperatures effectively:

- Importance of Temperature Control: Different types of food and cooking techniques require specific temperature ranges. Understanding the ideal temperature range for various cooking methods allows you to tailor your approach and achieve optimal results. Slow smoking requires lower temperatures for longer durations, while high-heat searing demands hotter temperatures for shorter periods.

- Digital Controller: The digital controller on your Traeger grill serves as the central hub for temperature regulation. It provides an intuitive interface for setting and adjusting the desired temperature. The digital display shows the current temperature, allowing you to monitor and make necessary adjustments throughout the cooking process. Precise temperature control gives you the flexibility to customize the heat level according to your specific cooking needs.

- Preheating: Preheating your Traeger grill before placing the food on the grates is recommended to ensure temperature stability. Preheating allows the grill to reach the desired temperature and ensures even heat distribution throughout the cooking chamber. This step is essential for consistent cooking results.

- Minimizing Lid Opening: It's important to avoid frequent opening of the grill lid during the cooking process. Opening the lid can cause temperature fluctuations and prolong the cooking time. Try to keep the lid closed as much as possible to maintain a stable cooking environment.

- Monitoring Food Temperature: Monitoring the internal temperature of the food is crucial for determining its doneness. Using an instant-read thermometer or a built-in meat probe, you can accurately measure the temperature of the food. This eliminates guesswork and ensures that your dishes are cooked to perfection.

- Regulating Airflow: Regulating the airflow within the grill can help control the intensity of the fire and manage heat levels. Adjusting the air vents or dampers allows you to increase or decrease airflow. Opening the vents increases airflow and raises temperatures, while closing them restricts airflow and lowers temperatures. Experiment with the vent settings to achieve the desired heat levels for different cooking techniques.

By understanding the significance of temperature control, effectively utilizing the digital controller, and implementing practical tips for maintaining optimal temperatures, you'll be able to achieve exceptional cooking results with your Traeger grill. Whether you're aiming for low and slow smoking or high-heat grilling, precise temperature control sets the stage for culinary success and ensures a memorable dining experience.

Tips for Temperature Control and Management

These practical tips for temperature control and management with your Traeger grill will help you achieve precise cooking results and elevate your grilling game:

- Preheating: Always preheat your Traeger grill before cooking. This ensures even heat distribution throughout the cooking chamber. Follow the recommended preheating time provided in your grill's manual for optimal results.

- Use the Digital Controller: Take advantage of the digital controller on your Traeger grill. Set the desired temperature using the intuitive controls and monitor the current temperature on the digital display. Make adjustments as needed to maintain the desired heat level throughout the cooking process.

- Avoid Frequent Lid Opening: Limit lid openings to essential tasks such as flipping or checking on the food. Each time the lid is opened, heat escapes, and the internal temperature drops. Minimizing lid openings helps maintain consistent heat.

- Utilize Air Vents/Dampers: Adjust the air vents or dampers on your Traeger grill to control the airflow and manage heat levels. Opening the vents allows for increased airflow and higher temperatures, while closing them restricts airflow, resulting in lower temperatures. Find the right balance to maintain consistent heat.

- Monitor Food Temperature: Use an instant-read thermometer or a built-in meat probe to monitor the internal temperature of the food. This ensures that the food reaches the desired doneness without overcooking or undercooking. Insert the thermometer into the thickest part of the meat for accurate readings.

- Experiment with Pellet Types: Different wood pellet flavors can influence cooking temperature and add unique flavors to your food. Experiment with various pellet types to discover your preferred flavors and their effects on temperature control. Keep in mind that denser pellet types may burn slower, affecting temperature management.

- Plan for Resting Time: Allow your cooked food to rest for a few minutes before serving. During this time, the internal temperature continues to rise, and the flavors settle, resulting in juicier and more tender meat.

- Practice and Observe: Temperature control is a skill that develops with practice. Observe how your grill responds to temperature changes and become familiar with the nuances of temperature management on your specific Traeger model.

By implementing these tips, you'll enhance your temperature control and management skills, enabling you to achieve precise cooking results and impress your family and friends with exceptional dishes from your Traeger grill. Remember to practice, observe, and experiment to become a master of temperature control.

Grilling Techniques and Methods

Here's an elaborate exploration of various grilling techniques and methods that will help you unlock a wide range of culinary possibilities and create delicious grilled dishes with your Traeger grill:

- Direct Grilling: This is the most basic and common grilling method. Place the food directly over high heat and cook it directly. Ideal for quick-cooking foods like steaks, burgers, chicken breasts, and vegetables. Direct grilling creates a seared exterior and a juicy interior.

- Indirect Grilling: Cook the food next to, rather than directly over, the heat source. Suitable for larger cuts of meat like roasts, whole chickens, and ribs that require longer cooking times at lower temperatures. Indirect grilling allows for gentle, slow cooking, resulting in tender and juicy results.

- Smoking: Infuse food with rich, smoky flavors by cooking it at low temperatures (usually between 225°F and 275°F) over a longer period. Wood pellets or chips produce smoke that flavors the food. Popular for meats like brisket, ribs, pulled pork, and salmon. Requires patience and careful temperature control.

- Reverse Searing: Slow-cook thicker cuts of meat at a low temperature first (often through indirect grilling or smoking) until they reach the desired internal temperature. Finish by searing over high heat for a short period to create a caramelized crust. This technique ensures a uniformly cooked and flavorful piece of meat.

- Rotisserie: Utilize a rotisserie attachment on your Traeger grill for even cooking and browning of larger cuts of meat. Skewer the food onto a rotating spit, ensuring even heat distribution and basting in its own juices. Results in tender, succulent meat with a crispy and evenly browned exterior.

- Plank Grilling: Cook food on a pre-soaked wooden plank (typically cedar or oak). The plank imparts a unique smoky flavor and helps keep delicate fish moist and tender. Popular for grilling fish, such as salmon.

- Grilling with Cast Iron: Use cast iron cookware like griddles and skillets on your Traeger grill. Cast iron retains heat well and provides excellent heat distribution, allowing for searing, sautéing, and even baking on the grill. Perfect for delicate items like seafood, stir-fried vegetables, and baking biscuits or cornbread.

- Kebab Skewering: Skewer pieces of meat, seafood, and vegetables for easy flipping and even cooking. Marinate the ingredients beforehand or brush them with sauces during grilling for added taste. Kebab skewering is a versatile and interactive way to enjoy a variety of grilled foods.

Mastering these grilling techniques and methods will elevate your outdoor cooking game with your Traeger grill. Experiment with different methods, adjust cooking times and temperatures, and get creative with flavors and ingredients. With practice and a sense of adventure, you'll become a grilling expert capable of producing mouthwatering meals that impress your family and friends.

Wood Pellet Selection and Flavor Profiles

Choosing the right wood pellets for your Traeger grill is crucial in enhancing the flavor profile of your grilled dishes. Each type of wood pellet imparts a distinct aroma and taste, allowing you to customize your grilling experience based on your preferences and the specific flavors you want to achieve. Here's an elaboration on wood pellet selection and their corresponding flavor profiles:

- Hickory: Hickory wood pellets offer a robust and smoky flavor. They are ideal for grilling pork, beef, poultry, and game meats. The rich and slightly sweet flavor of hickory adds depth and complexity to your grilled dishes, creating a classic barbecue taste.

- Mesquite: Mesquite wood pellets provide a strong and distinctive smoky flavor. This bold flavor profile pairs well with beef, especially cuts like brisket and steaks. Mesquite imparts a rich, earthy taste that is particularly popular in southwestern and Tex-Mex cuisine.

- Apple: Apple wood pellets offer a subtly sweet and fruity flavor, making them suitable for a wide range of meats, including poultry, pork, and fish. The mild smoke from apple wood creates a delicate and slightly sweet taste, enhancing the natural flavors of the food without overpowering them.

- Cherry: Cherry wood pellets provide a slightly sweet and fruity flavor that complements a variety of meats, including pork, beef, poultry, and game. The mild smoke of cherry wood adds a touch of sweetness and imparts a reddish hue to the meat, making it visually appealing as well.

- Maple: Maple wood pellets contribute a mild and sweet flavor to your grilled dishes. They are excellent for grilling poultry, pork, and vegetables. The subtle smokiness of maple wood enhances the natural flavors of the food without overpowering them, resulting in a well-balanced and slightly sweet taste.

- Pecan: Pecan wood pellets offer a rich and nutty flavor that pairs well with a wide range of meats, including poultry, pork, and beef. The mild and slightly sweet smokiness of pecan wood adds depth and complexity to your grilled dishes, creating a well-rounded and aromatic flavor profile.

- Oak: Oak wood pellets provide a versatile and medium-bodied flavor that works well with various meats, including beef, poultry, and fish. The moderate smoke of oak wood enhances the natural flavors of the food without overpowering them, allowing the ingredients to shine through.

- Alder: Alder wood pellets offer a delicate and slightly sweet flavor that is particularly suited for grilling fish, seafood, and poultry. The light smoke of alder wood complements the delicate flavors of these ingredients, providing a subtle smokiness without overpowering the natural taste.

Remember, the choice of wood pellets greatly influences the overall flavor profile of your grilled dishes. Feel free to experiment with different wood pellet combinations to create your own unique flavors and aromas. Whether you prefer a bold and robust taste or a more subtle and sweet undertone, selecting the right wood pellets will elevate your grilling experience and help you achieve delicious and well-balanced results.

Cleaning and Maintenance

Proper cleaning and maintenance of your Traeger grill are essential for its longevity and optimal performance. Regular maintenance ensures a safe and hygienic cooking environment and helps preserve the quality of your grilled dishes. Here are some elaborated cleaning and maintenance tips for your Traeger grill:

- Regular Cleaning: Clean your Traeger grill after each use to prevent the buildup of grease, food particles, and ash. Allow the grill to cool down completely before cleaning. Use a grill brush or scraper to remove residue from the grates.

Wipe the interior surfaces, including the drip tray and grease bucket, with a damp cloth or paper towels. For stubborn residue, you can use warm soapy water or a non-abrasive grill cleaner.

- Deep Cleaning: Perform a deep cleaning of your Traeger grill at regular intervals, typically every few months or as needed. Remove the grates and clean them thoroughly with warm soapy water, scrubbing off any accumulated grease or residue. Empty and clean the drip tray, grease bucket, and heat baffle. Use a vacuum or brush to remove ash and debris from the firepot and interior chamber.

- Grease Management: Keep an eye on the grease buildup in the drip tray and grease bucket. Empty the grease bucket regularly to avoid overflow and potential fire hazards. Replace the drip tray liner as needed. Consider using a disposable aluminum foil drip tray liner for easier cleanup.

- Check the Auger and Hopper: Inspect the auger and hopper regularly to ensure they are clean and free from any blockages. Remove any debris or wood pellets that may have accumulated. This ensures smooth pellet feeding and consistent heat output during grilling.

- Clean the Exterior: Wipe down the exterior surfaces of your Traeger grill with a mild soapy water solution or stainless steel cleaner. Use a non-abrasive cloth or sponge to remove grease, stains, or fingerprints. Rinse and dry thoroughly to prevent water spots or corrosion.

- Check for Wear and Tear: Routinely inspect the components of your Traeger grill for signs of wear and tear. Check the gaskets, seals, and hinges for tightness and integrity. Replace any damaged or worn-out parts promptly to maintain the grill's efficiency and safety.

- Store Properly: If you plan to store your Traeger grill for an extended period, clean it thoroughly and ensure it is completely dry to prevent rusting. Cover the grill with a Traeger grill cover or a waterproof cover to protect it from the elements.

- Follow Manufacturer's Instructions: Always refer to the manufacturer's instructions and guidelines for specific cleaning and maintenance procedures for your Traeger grill model. They may provide additional recommendations or precautions to ensure the best care for your grill.

By following these cleaning and maintenance practices, you'll keep your Traeger grill in top condition, prolong its lifespan, and continue enjoying delicious grilled meals for years to come. Regular maintenance enhances the performance and longevity of your grill and contributes to a safe and enjoyable grilling experience.

Troubleshooting

While Traeger grills are generally reliable and perform well, there are some common faults or issues that you may encounter during your grilling sessions. Here's an elaboration on these common faults and troubleshooting tips for your Traeger grill:

- Failure to Ignite: Check power source, temperature dial, firepot cleanliness, pellet supply, and electrical connections.

- Inconsistent Temperature: Verify proper probe placement, clean temperature sensor, ensure unobstructed vents, adjust settings.

- Pellet Jamming: Remove blockages, avoid overfilling hopper, clean auger, lubricate for smooth operation.

- Excessive Smoke: Check wood pellet type and moisture level, adjust temperature settings, clean firepot.

- Uneven Heat Distribution: Ensure unobstructed grates, clean thoroughly, adjust food placement.

- Error Codes: Refer to user manual or contact Traeger customer support for guidance.

Always refer to the manufacturer's instructions and guidelines for detailed troubleshooting steps specific to your Traeger grill model. If needed, Traeger's customer support team is available to provide assistance and guidance in addressing any faults or concerns you may encounter.

The Important Matters

When using your Traeger grill, there are several important matters that require attention to ensure safe and optimal grilling results. Here's an elaboration on these matters:

1. Safety Precautions:
- Follow the manufacturer's instructions and safety guidelines to prevent accidents or injuries.
- Keep children and pets away from the grill while it's in use and during the cooling process.
- Use heat-resistant gloves or mitts when handling hot surfaces or accessories.

2. Proper Ventilation:
- Position your Traeger grill in a well-ventilated area, preferably outdoors or in a well-ventilated space.
- Proper ventilation allows for the release of smoke and combustion byproducts and reduces the risk of carbon monoxide buildup.
- Avoid using the grill in enclosed spaces or near flammable materials.

3. Pellet Storage:
- Store wood pellets in a dry and secure location, away from moisture and pests.
- Use airtight containers or bags to maintain pellet freshness.
- Avoid exposing pellets to direct sunlight or extreme temperatures.

4. Temperature Monitoring:
- Monitor the temperature of your Traeger grill throughout the cooking process.
- Use a reliable meat thermometer to monitor the internal temperature of meats for desired doneness.
- Regularly check the grill's temperature settings and make adjustments as needed to maintain consistent heat.

5. Pellet Hopper Management:
- Maintain an adequate supply of wood pellets in the hopper during grilling.
- Avoid running out of pellets, as it may result in a loss of heat and interrupt the cooking process.
- Follow the manufacturer's recommendations for pellet loading and avoid overfilling the hopper to prevent pellet jamming.

6. Regular Inspection:
- Periodically inspect your Traeger grill for signs of damage, wear, or malfunctioning components.
- Check electrical connections, cords, and plugs for signs of fraying or damage.
- Inspect grill grates, drip tray, and interior surfaces for cleanliness and functionality.
- Address any issues promptly to prevent further damage or safety hazards.

7. Follow Recipe Guidelines:
- Adhere to recommended cooking times, temperatures, and techniques when using recipes or following cooking instructions.
- Different cuts of meat and ingredients may require specific cooking approaches.
- Pay attention to recommended pellet flavor pairings for optimal taste and flavor enhancement.

8. Seasoning the Grill:
- Properly season your Traeger grill before its initial use or after an extended period of non-use.
- Seasoning helps burn off residual manufacturing oils or contaminants and creates a non-stick surface.
- Refer to the manufacturer's instructions on how to season your specific model.

9. Cleaning and Maintenance:
- Regularly clean and maintain your Traeger grill as outlined in the manufacturer's instructions.
- This includes cleaning grates, interior surfaces, drip tray, and grease management components.
- Keep the grill free from grease buildup and ash accumulation to ensure optimal performance and prevent fire hazards.

CHAPTER 2

BEEF, PORK, & LAMB

REVERSE-SEARED TRI-TIP STEAK

Prep Time: 10 minutes | Smoking Time: 2 to 3 hours | Serves 4

INGREDIENTS

- 1½ pounds tri-tip steak
- 1 batch Espresso Brisket Rub

The reverse-sear method involves slow smoking the steak before finishing it with a high-heat sear. This technique results in a perfectly cooked, juicy, and flavorful tri-tip steak. Enjoy!

INSTRUCTIONS

1. Prepare your Traeger grill by supplying it with wood pellets and following the start-up procedure. Preheat the grill, with the lid closed, to 180°F.
2. Season the tri-tip steak with the Espresso Brisket Rub, ensuring it is evenly coated. Allow the steak to sit at room temperature for about 10 minutes.
3. Place the seasoned tri-tip steak directly on the grill grate and smoke it until the internal temperature reaches 140°F. This slow smoking process will infuse the steak with delicious smoky flavor.
4. Increase the grill's temperature to 450°F and continue cooking the steak until the internal temperature reaches 145°F for medium-rare doneness.
5. Once the desired temperature is reached, remove the tri-tip steak from the grill and let it rest for 10 minutes. This allows the juices to redistribute and ensures a tender and flavorful steak.
6. After resting, slice the tri-tip steak against the grain into thin slices.
7. Serve the reverse-seared tri-tip steak as a main course or in sandwiches, tacos, or salads.

GRILLED VENISON STEAKS

Prep Time: 10 minutes | Grilling Time: 8 to 10 minutes | Serves 4

INGREDIENTS

- 4 venison steaks
- 2 tablespoons olive oil
- Salt and pepper, to taste
- Optional: your choice of seasonings or marinade

Venison is a lean meat, so be careful not to overcook it to prevent it from becoming tough. Adjust the cooking time based on the thickness of the steaks and your preferred level of doneness.

INSTRUCTIONS

1. Preheat your grill to medium-high heat.
2. Brush the venison steaks with olive oil and season them with salt, pepper, and any additional seasonings or marinade of your choice. Allow the steaks to sit at room temperature for about 10 minutes to absorb the flavors.
3. Place the venison steaks on the preheated grill and cook them for 4 to 5 minutes per side for medium-rare doneness. Adjust the cooking time based on your desired level of doneness.
4. Use a meat thermometer to check the internal temperature of the steaks. For medium-rare, the temperature should reach 135°F to 140°F.
5. Once cooked to your desired level of doneness, remove the venison steaks from the grill and let them rest for a few minutes. This allows the juices to redistribute and ensures tender and flavorful steaks.
6. Serve the grilled venison steaks hot with your favorite side dishes, such as roasted vegetables, mashed potatoes, or a fresh salad.
7. Enjoy the delicious flavors of grilled venison!

BBQ PULLED PORK

Prep Time: 15 minutes | Cook Time: 8-10 hours | Serves 6-8

INGREDIENTS

- 4-5 pounds pork shoulder or pork butt
- 2 tablespoons brown sugar
- 2 tablespoons paprika
- 1 tablespoon garlic powder
- 1 tablespoon onion powder
- 1 tablespoon salt
- 1 teaspoon black pepper
- 1 cup BBQ sauce (plus extra for serving)
- 1/2 cup apple cider vinegar
- 1/2 cup chicken broth

The long, slow cooking process ensures the pork shoulder becomes incredibly tender and develops rich flavors.

INSTRUCTIONS

1. In a small bowl, combine the brown sugar, paprika, garlic powder, onion powder, salt, and black pepper to create a dry rub.
2. Rub the dry rub mixture all over the pork shoulder, ensuring it is evenly coated.
3. Preheat your smoker or grill to 225°F (107°C) and set it up for indirect heat.
4. Place the seasoned pork shoulder directly on the smoker grates or in a roasting pan if using a grill.
5. Close the lid of the smoker or grill and cook the pork shoulder low and slow for 8-10 hours, or until the internal temperature reaches 195-205°F (90-96°C) and the meat is tender and easily pulled apart with a fork.
6. In a small bowl, mix together the BBQ sauce, apple cider vinegar, and chicken broth to create a basting sauce. Once the pork shoulder reaches the desired temperature, baste it generously with the sauce mixture and continue cooking for an additional 30 minutes to allow the flavors to meld.
7. Remove the pork shoulder from the smoker or grill and let it rest for a few minutes.
8. Using two forks or meat claws, shred the pork shoulder into small pieces.

SMOKED PEPPERONI CALZONES

Prep Time: 20 minutes | Cook Time: 25-30 minutes | Serves 4

INGREDIENTS

- 1 pound pizza dough
- 1 cup marinara sauce
- 2 cups shredded mozzarella cheese
- 1 cup sliced pepperoni
- 1/2 cup diced bell peppers
- 1/4 cup diced onions
- 1/4 cup sliced black olives
- 1 tablespoon olive oil
- 1 teaspoon dried oregano
- Salt and pepper to taste

Keep an eye on the calzones and adjust the cooking time if needed to achieve your desired level of crispiness and doneness.

INSTRUCTIONS

1. Preheat your Traeger grill to 400°F (200°C).
2. Divide the pizza dough into 4 equal portions and roll each portion into a circle or oval shape.
3. In a bowl, mix together the marinara sauce, mozzarella cheese, pepperoni, bell peppers, onions, and black olives. Season with salt, pepper, and dried oregano.
4. Spoon the filling onto one half of each dough portion, leaving a border around the edges.
5. Fold the other half of the dough over the filling and pinch the edges to seal the calzones.
6. Brush the tops of the calzones with olive oil and sprinkle with a pinch of salt and dried oregano.
7. Place the calzones directly on the grill grate and close the lid. Cook for 25-30 minutes or until the calzones are golden brown and the cheese is melted.
8. Remove the calzones from the grill and let them cool for a few minutes before serving. Enjoy!

BACON-WRAPPED VENISON BACKSTRAP

Prep Time: 15 minutes | Cook Time: 25-30 minutes | Serving Size: 4 servings

INGREDIENTS

- 2 pounds venison backstrap (deer loin)
- 8 slices bacon
- 2 tablespoons olive oil
- 2 cloves garlic, minced
- 1 teaspoon dried thyme
- Salt and pepper to taste

Cooking times may vary depending on the thickness of the venison backstrap and the temperature of your Traeger grill. Use a meat thermometer to check the internal temperature of the meat to ensure it reaches your preferred level of doneness. Adjust the cooking time as needed.

INSTRUCTIONS

1. Preheat your Traeger grill to 375°F (190°C).
2. Season the venison backstrap with olive oil, minced garlic, dried thyme, salt, and pepper. Let it marinate for 10 minutes.
3. Wrap each slice of bacon around the venison backstrap, securing it with toothpicks if needed.
4. Place the bacon-wrapped backstrap directly on the grill grate and close the lid. Cook for 25-30 minutes or until the bacon is crispy and the internal temperature of the meat reaches your desired level of doneness (medium-rare is recommended for venison).
5. Remove the backstrap from the grill and let it rest for a few minutes before slicing. Remove the toothpicks and slice the backstrap into medallions. Serve and enjoy!

PERFECT ROAST PRIME RIB

Prep Time: 10 minutes | Cook Time: Varies | Serves 6-8

INGREDIENTS

- Prime rib roast
- 2 tablespoons olive oil
- 2 tablespoons minced garlic
- 2 tablespoons chopped fresh rosemary
- Salt and pepper to taste

It's important to monitor the internal temperature of the prime rib using a meat thermometer to ensure it reaches your desired level of doneness. Adjust the cooking time as needed based on the weight of the roast and your preferred level of doneness.

INSTRUCTIONS

1. Preheat your Traeger grill to 225°F (107°C).
2. Rub the prime rib roast with olive oil, minced garlic, chopped fresh rosemary, salt, and pepper. Ensure the entire surface is evenly coated.
3. Place the prime rib roast directly on the grill grate with the fat side up. Insert a meat probe into the thickest part of the roast, making sure it doesn't touch the bone.
4. Close the lid and cook the prime rib at 225°F (107°C) until the internal temperature reaches your desired level of doneness. The general guideline is approximately 20 minutes per pound for medium-rare.
5. Once the prime rib reaches the desired temperature, remove it from the grill and let it rest for 15-20 minutes before carving. This allows the juices to redistribute.
6. Slice the prime rib into thick slices and serve. Enjoy your perfectly cooked roast prime rib!

SMOKED SAUSAGE LASAGNA

Prep Time: 30 minutes | Cook Time: 1 hour 30 minutes | Serving Size: 8 servings

INGREDIENTS

- 1 pound smoked sausage, sliced

- 1 onion, chopped

- 3 cloves garlic, minced

- 1 can (28 ounces) crushed tomatoes

- 1 can (6 ounces) tomato paste

- 2 teaspoons dried basil

- 2 teaspoons dried oregano

- 1 teaspoon sugar

- Salt and pepper to taste

- 2 cups shredded mozzarella cheese

- 1 cup grated Parmesan cheese

 Cooking times may vary depending on the specific temperature and heat distribution of your Traeger grill.

INSTRUCTIONS

1. Preheat your Traeger grill to 375°F (190°C).

2. In a large skillet, cook the sliced smoked sausage over medium heat until lightly browned. Remove the sausage from the skillet and set it aside.

3. In the same skillet, sauté the chopped onion and minced garlic until softened.

4. Add the crushed tomatoes, tomato paste, dried basil, dried oregano, sugar, salt, and pepper to the skillet. Stir well to combine and simmer for 10-15 minutes.

5. Spread a thin layer of the tomato sauce on the bottom of a deep baking dish.

6. Arrange 4 cooked lasagna noodles over the sauce, followed by a layer of the cooked sausage slices. Top with a layer of mozzarella cheese and Parmesan cheese.

7. Repeat the layers with the remaining ingredients, finishing with a layer of sauce and cheese on top.

8. Place the baking dish directly on the grill grate and close the lid. Bake for 1 hour 30 minutes or until the lasagna is bubbling and the cheese is golden brown.

9. Remove the lasagna from the grill and let it cool for a few minutes. Garnish with fresh basil leaves if desired. Serve and enjoy!

BBQ BREAKFAST GRITS WITH SMOKED FLAVOR

Prep Time: 10 minutes | Cook Time: 1 hour | Serving Size: 4 servings

INGREDIENTS

- 1 cup stone-ground grits

- 4 cups water

- 1 cup milk

- 4 tablespoons butter

- 1 cup shredded cheddar cheese

- 4 slices cooked bacon, crumbled

- 2 green onions, chopped

- Salt and pepper to taste

 Cooking times may vary depending on the specific temperature and heat distribution of your Traeger grill. Keep an eye on the grits and adjust the cooking time if needed to ensure they are cooked to your desired consistency.

INSTRUCTIONS

1. Preheat your Traeger grill to 225°F (107°C).

2. In a large saucepan, bring the water to a boil. Slowly stir in the grits and reduce the heat to low.

3. Cook the grits for about 30-40 minutes, stirring occasionally, until they become thick and creamy.

4. Stir in the milk, butter, shredded cheddar cheese, crumbled bacon, and chopped green onions. Season with salt and pepper to taste.

5. Transfer the mixture to a cast-iron skillet or a heatproof dish.

6. Place the skillet or dish directly on the grill grate and close the lid. Cook for 20-30 minutes or until the grits are heated through and the cheese is melted and bubbly.

7. Remove from the grill and let it cool for a few minutes before serving. Serve the BBQ breakfast grits as a delicious and flavorful side dish. Enjoy!

BEER-BRINED VENISON RACK

Prep time: 15 minutes | Cook time: 30-40 minutes | Serves: 4-6

INGREDIENTS

- 1 venison rack (about 2-3 pounds)

- 4 cups beer (such as ale or lager)

- 1/2 cup soy sauce

- 1/4 cup brown sugar

- 4 cloves garlic, minced

- 2 tablespoons Dijon mustard

- 2 tablespoons Worcestershire sauce

- 1 tablespoon black peppercorns

- 1 tablespoon dried rosemary

- 1 tablespoon vegetable oil

Cooking times may vary depending on the thickness of the venison rack and the heat of your grill. Use a meat thermometer to ensure the desired level of doneness is reached.

INSTRUCTIONS

1. In a large bowl or resealable bag, combine the beer, soy sauce, brown sugar, minced garlic, Dijon mustard, Worcestershire sauce, black peppercorns, and dried rosemary. Stir or shake well to dissolve the brown sugar.

2. Place the venison rack in the brine mixture, ensuring it is fully submerged. If needed, add more beer or water to cover the meat. Seal the bag or cover the bowl and refrigerate for at least 4 hours or overnight.

3. Preheat your Traeger grill according to the manufacturer's instructions. Set the temperature to 400°F.

4. Remove the venison rack from the brine and pat it dry with paper towels. Discard the brine.

5. Rub the venison rack with vegetable oil and season it generously with salt and freshly ground black pepper.

6. Place the venison rack directly on the grill grate, bone side down. Close the lid and cook for 30-40 minutes, or until the internal temperature reaches 135°F for medium-rare.

7. Remove the venison rack from the grill and let it rest for 10 minutes before carving.

ROSEMARY-SMOKED LAMB CHOPS WITH AROMATIC HERBS

Prep Time: 10 minutes | Cook Time: 20-25 minutes | Serving Size: 4 servings

INGREDIENTS

- 8 lamb chops

- 2 tablespoons olive oil

- 4 cloves garlic, minced

- 2 tablespoons chopped fresh rosemary

- 1 tablespoon chopped fresh thyme

- 1 teaspoon dried oregano

- Salt and pepper to taste

Cooking times may vary depending on the thickness of the lamb chops and your preferred level of doneness. Use a meat thermometer to check the internal temperature of the lamb chops for accuracy. Adjust the cooking time as needed.

INSTRUCTIONS

1. Preheat your Traeger grill to 225°F (107°C).

2. In a small bowl, mix together the olive oil, minced garlic, chopped fresh rosemary, chopped fresh thyme, dried oregano, salt, and pepper to create a marinade.

3. Rub the lamb chops with the marinade, ensuring all sides are coated. Let them marinate for at least 10 minutes.

4. Place the lamb chops directly on the grill grate and close the lid. Smoke the chops at 225°F (107°C) for 15 minutes.

5. After 15 minutes, increase the temperature to 375°F (190°C) and continue cooking for an additional 5-10 minutes or until the lamb chops reach your desired level of doneness (medium-rare is recommended for lamb).

6. Remove the lamb chops from the grill and let them rest for a few minutes before serving.

7. Serve the smoked lamb chops with your choice of side dishes or sauces. Enjoy the flavorful and aromatic herb-infused lamb chops!

APPLE-STUFFED PORK LOIN WITH TRAEGER GRILL

Prep Time: 30 minutes I Cook Time: 1 hour 30 minutes I Serving Size: 6 servings

INGREDIENTS

- 1 (3-4 pound) pork loin roast
- 2 tablespoons olive oil
- 2 teaspoons dried thyme
- 2 teaspoons dried rosemary
- Salt and pepper to taste
- 2 apples, peeled, cored, thinly sliced
- 1/2 cup breadcrumbs
- 2 tablespoons brown sugar
- 1 tablespoon melted butter

 Use a meat thermometer to check the internal temperature of the pork loin to ensure it reaches the recommended safe temperature. Adjust the cooking time as needed.

INSTRUCTIONS

1. Preheat your Traeger grill to 375°F (190°C).
2. Butterfly the pork loin roast by making a lengthwise cut down the center, stopping about 1/2 inch from the bottom.
3. Open up the pork loin and flatten it with a meat mallet to an even thickness.
4. In a small bowl, combine the olive oil, dried thyme, dried rosemary, salt, and pepper. Rub the mixture all over the pork loin, ensuring it is well-coated.
5. In a separate bowl, mix together the sliced apples, breadcrumbs, brown sugar, and melted butter.
6. Spread the apple mixture evenly over the surface of the pork loin.
7. Roll up the pork loin tightly, starting from one end. Use butcher's twine to tie it at 1-inch intervals to secure the roll.
8. Place the stuffed pork loin directly on the grill grate, seam side down.
9. Close the lid and cook for 1 hour 30 minutes, or until the internal temperature of the pork loin reaches 145°F (63°C).
10. Remove the pork loin from the grill and let it rest for 10 minutes before slicing.

SMOKY BABY BACK RIBS

Prep Time: 15 minutes I Cook Time: 4-5 hours I Serving Size: 4 servings

INGREDIENTS

- 2 racks of baby back ribs
- 1/4 cup brown sugar
- 2 tablespoons paprika
- 1 tablespoon chili powder
- 1 tablespoon garlic powder
- 1 tablespoon onion powder
- 1 tablespoon salt
- 1 tablespoon black pepper
- BBQ sauce of your choice

 Cooking times may vary depending on the thickness of the ribs and your desired level of tenderness. Use a meat thermometer to check the internal temperature of the ribs to ensure they are cooked to your liking. Adjust the cooking time as needed.

INSTRUCTIONS

1. Preheat your Traeger grill to 225°F (107°C).
2. In a bowl, combine the brown sugar, paprika, chili powder, garlic powder, onion powder, salt, black pepper, and cayenne pepper (if using) to create a dry rub.
3. Remove the membrane from the back of the ribs, if desired, by lifting a corner with a knife and then pulling it off with a paper towel.
4. Apply the dry rub generously on both sides of the ribs, pressing it into the meat.
5. Place the ribs directly on the grill grate, bone side down.
6. Close the lid and smoke the ribs at 225°F (107°C) for 4-5 hours, or until the meat is tender and pulls away from the bone.
7. Optionally, during the last 30 minutes of cooking, brush the ribs with your favorite BBQ sauce for added flavor and caramelization.
8. Remove the ribs from the grill and let them rest for a few minutes before cutting into individual ribs. Serve with additional BBQ sauce on the side. Enjoy the smoky and tender baby back ribs!

CHEESEBURGER HAND PIES

Prep Time: 20 minutes | Cook Time: 20 minutes | Serving Size: 4 hand pies

INGREDIENTS

- 1 pound ground beef
- 1/2 onion, finely chopped
- 1 clove garlic, minced
- 2 tablespoons ketchup
- 2 tablespoons mustard
- 1 tablespoon Worcestershire sauce
- Salt and pepper to taste
- 1 package refrigerated pie crusts
- 4 slices American cheese
- 1 egg, beaten (for egg wash)

 Keep an eye on the hand pies and adjust the cooking time if needed to ensure they are cooked to your desired level of doneness and the crust is golden brown.

INSTRUCTIONS

1. Preheat your Traeger grill to 375°F (190°C).
2. In a skillet over medium heat, cook the ground beef, chopped onion, and minced garlic until the beef is browned and the onion is softened. Drain any excess fat.
3. Stir in the ketchup, mustard, Worcestershire sauce, salt, and pepper. Cook for an additional 2-3 minutes, then remove from heat.
4. Roll out the refrigerated pie crusts on a lightly floured surface. Cut each crust into 4 equal-sized squares.
5. Place a spoonful of the ground beef mixture on one half of each square. Top with a slice of American cheese.
6. Fold the other half of the crust over the filling, creating a triangle shape. Use a fork to seal the edges.
7. Place the hand pies directly on the grill grate and close the lid. Cook for 20 minutes or until the crust is golden brown.
8. Remove the hand pies from the grill and let them cool for a few minutes before serving.

BACON-SWISS CHEESESTEAK MEATLOAF

Prep Time: 20 minutes | Cook Time: 1 hour | Serving Size: 6 servings

INGREDIENTS

- 1 ½ pounds ground beef
- 1 cup diced onions
- 1 cup diced green bell peppers
- 2 cloves garlic, minced
- 1 cup breadcrumbs
- 2 eggs, lightly beaten
- 1 tablespoon Worcestershire sauce
- 1 teaspoon salt
- 1 teaspoon black pepper
- 8 slices Swiss cheese
- 8 slices bacon

 You can customize this recipe by adding other ingredients like sautéed onions, peppers, or mushrooms to enhance the flavor.

INSTRUCTIONS

1. Preheat your oven to 350°F (175°C) and lightly grease a loaf pan.
2. In a large bowl, combine the ground beef, ground pork, breadcrumbs, diced onion, diced bell pepper, diced mushrooms, minced garlic, eggs, shredded Swiss cheese, crumbled bacon, Worcestershire sauce, salt, and black pepper. Mix well until all ingredients are evenly combined.
3. Transfer the meat mixture into the greased loaf pan, pressing it down firmly to shape it into a loaf.
4. Spread the ketchup evenly over the top of the meatloaf.
5. Place the loaf pan in the preheated oven and bake for 1 hour, or until the internal temperature reaches 160°F (71°C).
6. Once cooked, remove the meatloaf from the oven and let it rest for a few minutes before slicing.
7. Slice the meatloaf into thick slices and serve hot.

CLASSIC BBQ BABY BACK RIBS

Prep Time: 15 minutes | Cook Time: 2-3 hours | Serves 4

INGREDIENTS

- 2 racks of baby back ribs
- 1/4 cup brown sugar
- 1 tablespoon paprika
- 1 tablespoon chili powder
- 1 tablespoon garlic powder
- 1 tablespoon onion powder
- 1 teaspoon salt
- 1 teaspoon black pepper
- 1 cup BBQ sauce

Cooking times may vary depending on the thickness of the ribs and the heat of your grill or smoker. Adjust cooking time accordingly to ensure the ribs are cooked to your desired tenderness.

INSTRUCTIONS

1. Preheat your grill or smoker to 225°F (107°C) and set it up for indirect heat.
2. In a small bowl, mix together the brown sugar, paprika, chili powder, garlic powder, onion powder, salt, and black pepper to create a dry rub.
3. Pat the ribs dry with paper towels. Remove the thin membrane on the back of the ribs by sliding a butter knife under it and then pulling it off.
4. Generously season both sides of the ribs with the dry rub, ensuring they are evenly coated.
5. Place the ribs bone-side down on the grill grates or in a rib rack if using a smoker.
6. Close the lid of the grill or smoker and cook the ribs low and slow for 2-3 hours, or until the meat is tender and starts to pull away from the bones.
7. During the last 30 minutes of cooking, baste the ribs with BBQ sauce, brushing it on both sides.
8. Remove the ribs from the grill or smoker and let them rest for a few minutes.
9. Cut the ribs into individual portions and serve with additional BBQ sauce on the side.

SMOKED RACK OF LAMB WITH HERB SEASONING

Prep Time: 15 minutes | Cook Time: 1 hour | Serving Size: 2 servings

INGREDIENTS

- 1 rack of lamb (8 chops)
- 2 tablespoons olive oil
- 2 cloves garlic, minced
- 1 teaspoon dried rosemary
- 1 teaspoon dried thyme
- 1 teaspoon dried oregano
- 1 teaspoon salt
- 1/2 teaspoon black pepper

Cooking times may vary depending on the size and thickness of the rack of lamb, as well as your desired level of doneness. Use a meat thermometer to check the internal temperature for accuracy.

INSTRUCTIONS

1. Preheat your Traeger grill to 225°F (107°C).
2. In a small bowl, combine the olive oil, minced garlic, dried rosemary, dried thyme, dried oregano, salt, and black pepper to create the herb seasoning mixture.
3. Pat the rack of lamb dry with paper towels. Trim any excess fat if desired.
4. Brush the herb seasoning mixture all over the rack of lamb, coating it evenly.
5. Place the rack of lamb directly on the grill grate, bone side down.
6. Close the lid and smoke the lamb at 225°F (107°C) for approximately 1 hour, or until the internal temperature reaches your desired doneness. For medium-rare, aim for an internal temperature of 135°F (57°C).
7. Remove the rack of lamb from the grill and let it rest for about 10 minutes before slicing.
8. Slice the rack of lamb into individual chops and serve. The smoky and herb-infused flavor will enhance the natural richness of the lamb.

SOUTHERN SUGAR-GLAZED HAM WITH SMOKY TWIST

Prep Time: 15 minutes I Cook Time: 2-3 hours I Serving Size: Varies based on ham size

INGREDIENTS

-- 1 fully cooked ham (bone-in or boneless)

- 1 cup brown sugar

- 1/2 cup honey

- 1/4 cup Dijon mustard

- 2 tablespoons apple cider vinegar

- 1 tablespoon smoked paprika

- 1 teaspoon garlic powder

- 1 teaspoon onion powder

- 1/2 teaspoon ground cinnamon

- 1/2 teaspoon ground cloves

- 1/2 teaspoon black pepper

QUICK TIPS
Basting the ham with the glaze towards the end of cooking will create a flavorful caramelized coating.

INSTRUCTIONS

1. Preheat your Traeger grill to 275°F (135°C).

2. In a bowl, combine the brown sugar, honey, Dijon mustard, apple cider vinegar, smoked paprika, garlic powder, onion powder, ground cinnamon, ground cloves, black pepper, and cayenne pepper (if using) to create the glaze mixture.

3. Score the surface of the ham in a crisscross pattern, about 1/4 inch deep. This will help the glaze penetrate the meat.

4. Place the ham directly on the grill grate.

5. Close the lid and smoke the ham at 275°F (135°C) for 2-3 hours, or until the internal temperature reaches 140°F (60°C).

6. During the last 30 minutes of cooking, brush the ham generously with the glaze mixture every 10 minutes.

7. Remove the ham from the grill and let it rest for a few minutes before carving.

8. Slice the ham and serve with any remaining glaze on the side.

9. Enjoy the Southern Sugar-Glazed Ham with its smoky and sweet flavors that are sure to be a hit at any gathering or special occasion.

KOREAN BBQ-STYLE PRIME RIBS

Prep Time: 15 minutes I Marinating Time: 4 hours I Cook Time: 20-30 minutes I Serves 4

INGREDIENTS

-- 2 racks of prime ribs

- 1/2 cup soy sauce

- 1/4 cup brown sugar

- 2 tablespoons sesame oil

- 4 cloves garlic, minced

- 1 tablespoon grated ginger

- 2 tablespoons rice vinegar

- 1 tablespoon Sriracha sauce

- 2 green onions, finely chopped

- Toasted sesame seeds

QUICK TIPS
Adjust the cooking time as needed. The marinade adds a savory and slightly sweet flavor to the prime ribs, while the high heat grilling creates a delicious charred exterior.

INSTRUCTIONS

1. Whisk together soy sauce, brown sugar, sesame oil, garlic, ginger, rice vinegar, and Sriracha.

2. Place the racks of prime ribs in a large resealable plastic bag or a shallow dish. Pour the marinade over the ribs, ensuring they are fully coated. Seal the bag or cover the dish and marinate in the refrigerator for at least 4 hours, or preferably overnight, to allow the flavors to infuse.

3. Preheat your Traeger grill to high heat or set it up for direct grilling at around 450°F (230°C).

4. Remove the prime ribs from the marinade, allowing any excess marinade to drip off.

5. Place the prime ribs directly on the grill grate and sear them for about 2-3 minutes per side, or until nicely browned.

6. Reduce the heat to medium and continue grilling the prime ribs for an additional 15-20 minutes, or until they reach your desired level of doneness. For medium-rare, aim for an internal temperature of around 130°F (54°C).

7. Remove the prime ribs from the grill and let them rest for a few minutes before slicing.

SMOKED HONEY-GLAZED HAM

Prep Time: 10 minutes Cook Time: 3-4 hours I Serving Size: Varies based on ham size

INGREDIENTS

- 1 fully cooked ham
- 1 cup honey
- 1/2 cup brown sugar
- 1/4 cup Dijon mustard
- 1/4 cup apple cider vinegar
- 1 teaspoon ground cloves
- 1 teaspoon ground cinnamon
- 1/2 teaspoon ground nutmeg

Cooking times may vary depending on the size of the ham and the temperature of your smoker. Use a meat thermometer to check the internal temperature for accuracy. Adjust the cooking time as needed.

INSTRUCTIONS

1. Preheat your smoker to 225°F (110°C).
2. In a bowl, combine the honey, brown sugar, Dijon mustard, apple cider vinegar, ground cloves, ground cinnamon, and ground nutmeg. Mix well to make the glaze.
3. Place the fully cooked ham on a wire rack or directly on the smoker grate.
4. Brush a generous amount of the glaze over the entire surface of the ham, making sure to coat it evenly.
5. Place the ham in the smoker and close the lid. Smoke the ham for 3-4 hours, or until the internal temperature reaches around 140°F (60°C).
6. Every 30 minutes, brush more glaze over the ham to create a sticky, caramelized crust.
7. Once the ham reaches the desired temperature, remove it from the smoker and let it rest for about 10-15 minutes before slicing.
8. Slice the smoked honey-glazed ham and serve it warm.

JALAPENO-BACON-WRAPPED PORK TENDERLOIN

Prep Time: 20 minutes I Cook Time: 30-35 minutes I Serving Size: 4 servings

INGREDIENTS

- 1 pork tenderloin (1 to 1.5 pounds)
- 6-8 slices of bacon
- 2 jalapeno peppers, seeded and sliced
- 2 tbsp brown sugar
- 1 tsp each garlic powder, smoked paprika
- 1/2 tsp each salt, black pepper

INSTRUCTIONS

1. Preheat Traeger grill to 375°F (190°C) for direct grilling.
2. Season pork tenderloin with salt, pepper, garlic powder, and smoked paprika.
3. Wrap bacon slices around jalapeno strips.
4. Wrap bacon-wrapped jalapenos around pork tenderloin.
5. Sprinkle with brown sugar, garlic powder, smoked paprika, salt, and black pepper.
6. Grill for 30-35 minutes until internal temperature reaches 145°F (63°C).
7. Let rest, remove toothpicks, and slice.

Cooking times may vary. Enjoy the flavorful jalapeno-bacon-wrapped pork tenderloin with your favorite sides.

SMOKED NEW YORK STRIP STEAKS

Prep Time: 15 minutes | Smoking Time: 1 to 2 hours | Serving Size: 4

INGREDIENTS

- 4 (1-inch-thick) New York strip steaks
- 2 tablespoons olive oil
- Salt
- Freshly ground black pepper

The smoking process infuses the steaks with a delicious smoky flavor, while the seasoning enhances their taste. Serve the smoked New York strip steaks with your favorite side dishes, such as grilled vegetables or mashed potatoes, for a satisfying meal.

INSTRUCTIONS

1. Preheat your Traeger grill according to the manufacturer's instructions. Close the lid and set the temperature to 180°F (82°C).
2. Rub the New York strip steaks with olive oil, ensuring they are coated evenly. Season both sides of the steaks with salt and freshly ground black pepper.
3. Place the steaks directly on the grill grate and close the lid. Smoke the steaks for 1 to 2 hours, depending on your desired level of smokiness and doneness. For a lighter smoke flavor, smoke for 1 hour. For a stronger smoke flavor, smoke for up to 2 hours.
4. After the desired smoking time, increase the grill's temperature to 375°F (190°C). Continue cooking the steaks until they reach an internal temperature of 145°F (63°C) for medium-rare. Use an instant-read thermometer to check the temperature.
5. Once the steaks have reached the desired doneness, remove them from the grill and let them rest for 5 minutes before slicing and serving.

HARISSA-GLAZED SMOKED SHORT RIBS

Prep Time: 20 minutes | Marinating Time: 4 hours | Cook Time: 4-5 hours | Serving Size: 4 servings

INGREDIENTS

- 2 racks of beef short ribs
- 1/4 cup harissa paste
- 2 tbsp each olive oil, honey, soy sauce
- 2 cloves garlic, minced
- 1 tbsp each ground cumin, paprika
- 1 tsp salt, 1/2 tsp black pepper
- Fresh cilantro or parsley, chopped (for garnish)

INSTRUCTIONS

1. Whisk harissa paste, olive oil, honey, soy sauce, minced garlic, cumin, paprika, salt, and black pepper in a bowl.
2. Coat short ribs with the marinade, refrigerate for 4 hours or overnight.
3. Preheat Traeger grill to 225°F (107°C) for indirect grilling.
4. Smoke ribs on grill for 4-5 hours until tender and internal temperature reaches 195°F (90°C).
5. Baste with remaining marinade during last hour of smoking.
6. Remove from grill, let rest, and slice between bones.
7. Garnish with fresh cilantro or parsley.
8. Serve with favorite sides.

Cooking times may vary. Use a meat thermometer for accuracy. Enjoy the spicy and smoky harissa-glazed smoked short ribs!

REVERSE-SEARED BBQ PORK CHOPS

Prep Time: 10 minutes I Cook Time: 30-40 minutes I Serving Size: 4 servings

INGREDIENTS

- 4 bone-in pork chops (about 1 inch thick)
- 2 tablespoons olive oil
- 2 teaspoons paprika
- 1 teaspoon garlic powder
- 1 teaspoon onion powder
- 1 teaspoon brown sugar
- 1/2 teaspoon salt
- 1/2 teaspoon black pepper
- BBQ sauce (for brushing)

INSTRUCTIONS

1. Preheat Traeger grill to 225°F (107°C) for indirect grilling.
2. Season pork chops with olive oil, paprika, garlic powder, onion powder, brown sugar, salt, and black pepper.
3. Smoke pork chops on grill for 20-30 minutes until internal temperature reaches 120°F (49°C).
4. Increase grill temperature to high heat or use separate grill/skillet for searing.
5. Sear pork chops for 2-3 minutes per side until internal temperature reaches 145°F (63°C).
6. Brush pork chops with BBQ sauce during searing.
7. Remove from heat, let rest for a few minutes, and serve.

QUICK TIPS Adjust cooking times based on thickness of pork chops. Enjoy the flavorful and tender reverse-seared BBQ pork chops!

GREEK–STYLE LEG OF LAMB

Prep Time: 15 minutes I Marinating Time: 4 hours I Cook Time: 2-3 hours I Serves: 6-8

INGREDIENTS

- 1 leg of lamb (about 5-6 pounds)
- 4 cloves garlic, minced
- 2 tablespoons fresh rosemary, chopped
- 2 tablespoons fresh oregano, chopped
- 1 lemon, juiced
- 1/4 cup olive oil
- 2 teaspoons salt
- 1 teaspoon black pepper
- Greek yogurt (for serving)
- Fresh mint leaves (for garnish)

INSTRUCTIONS

1. In a bowl, combine minced garlic, chopped rosemary, chopped oregano, lemon juice, olive oil, salt, and black pepper to create the marinade.
2. Place the leg of lamb in a large resealable plastic bag or a shallow dish. Pour the marinade over the lamb, ensuring it is fully coated. Seal the bag or cover the dish and marinate in the refrigerator for at least 4 hours, or preferably overnight, to allow the flavors to infuse.
3. Preheat your Traeger grill to 325°F (163°C) and set it up for indirect grilling.
4. Remove the leg of lamb from the marinade, allowing any excess marinade to drip off. Place the lamb directly on the grill grate, fat side up.
5. Close the lid and cook for 2-3 hours, or until the internal temperature reaches 145°F (63°C) for medium-rare or 160°F (71°C) for medium. Use a meat thermometer to check the temperature.
6. During the cooking process, periodically baste the lamb with the remaining marinade to keep it moist and add flavor.
7. Once the lamb reaches the desired temperature, remove it from the grill and let it rest for 15-20 minutes before carving.
8. Carve the lamb into thin slices and serve with Greek yogurt for dipping.

QUICK TIPS Cooking times may vary depending on the size and thickness of the leg of lamb and the temperature of your Traeger grill. Use a meat thermometer to check the internal temperature for accuracy.

SANTA MARIA STYLE TRI-TIP ROAST

Prep Time: 15 minutes | Marinating Time: 4 hours | Cook Time: 30-40 minutes | Serves: 4-6

INGREDIENTS

- 1 tri-tip roast (about 2-3 pounds)
- 2 tablespoons olive oil
- 2 tablespoons Worcestershire sauce
- 2 cloves garlic, minced
- 1 tablespoon smoked paprika
- 1 tablespoon ground black pepper
- 1 tablespoon kosher salt
- 1 teaspoon dried oregano
- 1 teaspoon dried thyme
- 1 teaspoon onion powder
- 1 teaspoon garlic powder

The Santa Maria-style marinade infuses the roast with smoky and savory flavors, resulting in a deliciously seasoned tri-tip roast.

INSTRUCTIONS

1. In a bowl, combine olive oil, Worcestershire sauce, minced garlic, smoked paprika, black pepper, kosher salt, dried oregano, dried thyme, onion powder, and garlic powder to create the marinade.
2. Place the tri-tip roast in a large resealable plastic bag or a shallow dish. Pour the marinade over the roast, ensuring it is fully coated. Seal the bag or cover the dish and marinate in the refrigerator for at least 4 hours, or preferably overnight.
3. Preheat your Traeger grill to high heat or set it up for direct grilling at around 450°F (230°C).
4. Remove the tri-tip roast from the marinade, allowing any excess marinade to drip off.
5. Place the roast directly on the grill grate, fat side down.
6. Close the lid and grill for about 10-15 minutes on each side, or until the internal temperature reaches 130°F (54°C) for medium-rare or 135°F (57°C) for medium.
7. Baste the roast with the remaining marinade periodically during the cooking process to enhance the flavors and keep the meat moist.

SMOKED TRI-TIP ROAST WITH FLAVORFUL SEASONINGS

Prep Time: 15 minutes | Smoking Time: 1.5 to 2 hours | Resting Time: 15 minutes | Serves: 4-6

INGREDIENTS

- 1 tri-tip roast (about 2-3 pounds)
- 2 tablespoons olive oil
- 2 tablespoons smoked paprika
- 1 tablespoon garlic powder
- 1 tablespoon onion powder
- 1 tablespoon ground black pepper
- 1 tablespoon kosher salt
- 1 teaspoon dried oregano
- 1 teaspoon dried thyme

The combination of flavorful seasonings and slow smoking gives the tri-tip roast a delicious and smoky taste.

INSTRUCTIONS

1. Preheat your Traeger grill to 225°F (107°C) and set it up for indirect grilling.
2. In a small bowl, combine smoked paprika, garlic powder, onion powder, black pepper, kosher salt, dried oregano, dried thyme, and cayenne pepper (if using). Mix well to create a flavorful rub.
3. Rub the tri-tip roast with olive oil, ensuring it is evenly coated.
4. Sprinkle the rub mixture over the entire surface of the tri-tip roast, pressing it into the meat to adhere.
5. Place the seasoned tri-tip roast directly on the grill grate, fat side up.
6. Close the lid and smoke the tri-tip roast for 1.5 to 2 hours, or until the internal temperature reaches 130°F (54°C) for medium-rare or 135°F (57°C) for medium. Use a meat thermometer to check the temperature.
7. Once the tri-tip roast reaches the desired temperature, remove it from the grill and let it rest for 15 minutes. This allows the juices to redistribute and the meat to become more tender.
8. Slice the tri-tip roast against the grain into thin slices.
9. Serve the smoked tri-tip roast with your favorite sides, such as roasted vegetables, mashed potatoes, or a fresh salad.

BBQ PULLED PORK

Prep Time: 15 minutes | Cook Time: 6-8 hours ; Serving Size: 8 servings

INGREDIENTS

- 4-5 pounds pork shoulder or pork butt
- 2 tablespoons brown sugar
- 2 teaspoons paprika
- 2 teaspoons garlic powder
- 2 teaspoons onion powder
- 1 teaspoon salt
- 1 teaspoon black pepper
- 1 cup barbecue sauce
- 1/2 cup apple cider vinegar
- 1/4 cup chicken broth or water

 The long, slow smoking process results in tender and flavorful pulled pork.

INSTRUCTIONS

1. In a small bowl, combine brown sugar, paprika, garlic powder, onion powder, salt, and black pepper to create a dry rub.
2. Trim any excess fat from the pork shoulder or pork butt, if desired.
3. Rub the dry rub mixture all over the pork, making sure to coat it evenly.
4. Preheat your Traeger grill to 225°F (107°C) and set it up for indirect grilling.
5. Place the seasoned pork on the grill grate, fat side up.
6. Close the lid and smoke the pork for 6-8 hours, or until it reaches an internal temperature of around 195°F (90°C) and is tender enough to be easily shredded with a fork.
7. While the pork is smoking, prepare the barbecue sauce mixture. In a small saucepan, combine barbecue sauce, apple cider vinegar, and chicken broth or water. Heat the mixture over medium heat until warmed through.
8. Once the pork is done, remove it from the grill and let it rest for a few minutes.
9. Using two forks, shred the smoked pork, discarding any excess fat or bones.
10. Pour the barbecue sauce mixture over the shredded pork and mix well to coat.
11. Serve the BBQ pulled pork on hamburger buns or sandwich rolls.

SMOKY AND TENDER SPARE RIBS

Prep Time: 15 minutes | Cook Time: 4-5 hours | Serving Size: 4 servings

INGREDIENTS

- 2 racks of spare ribs
- 2 tablespoons brown sugar
- 2 teaspoons paprika
- 2 teaspoons garlic powder
- 2 teaspoons onion powder
- 1 teaspoon salt
- 1 teaspoon black pepper
- BBQ sauce, for basting and serving

 The low and slow smoking method infuses the spare ribs with smoky flavor and results in tender meat that is perfect for BBQ lovers.

INSTRUCTIONS

1. Preheat your Traeger grill to 225°F (107°C) and set it up for indirect grilling.
2. In a small bowl, combine brown sugar, paprika, garlic powder, onion powder, salt, and black pepper to create a dry rub.
3. Remove the membrane from the back of the spare ribs by using a knife to loosen one end, then gripping it with a paper towel and peeling it off.
4. Rub the dry rub mixture all over the spare ribs, making sure to coat them evenly.
5. Place the spare ribs directly on the grill grate, bone side down.
6. Close the lid and smoke the ribs for 4-5 hours, or until they are tender and the meat pulls away from the bones.
7. Every hour, baste the spare ribs with BBQ sauce to add flavor and moisture. Use your favorite BBQ sauce or make your own.
8. During the last 30 minutes of cooking, increase the grill temperature to 275°F (135°C) to help caramelize the BBQ sauce.
9. Once the spare ribs are done, remove them from the grill and let them rest for a few minutes.
10. Cut the spare ribs into individual portions and serve with additional BBQ sauce on the side.

GRILLED LONDON BROIL

Prep Time: 10 minutes | Marinating Time: 2 hours | Cook Time: 10-15 minutes | Serves 4

INGREDIENTS

- 2 pounds London broil steak
- 1/4 cup soy sauce
- 2 tablespoons Worcestershire sauce
- 2 tablespoons olive oil
- 2 cloves garlic, minced
- 1 tablespoon Dijon mustard
- 1 teaspoon dried thyme
- 1 teaspoon black pepper
- 1/2 teaspoon salt

The marinade adds flavor and tenderness to the steak, while the high heat grilling creates a delicious charred exterior. Enjoy the grilled London broil as a flavorful and satisfying meal.

INSTRUCTIONS

1. In a bowl, whisk together soy sauce, Worcestershire sauce, olive oil, minced garlic, Dijon mustard, dried thyme, black pepper, and salt to create the marinade.
2. Place the London broil steak in a large resealable plastic bag or a shallow dish. Pour the marinade over the steak, making sure it is fully coated. Seal the bag or cover the dish and marinate in the refrigerator for at least 2 hours, or preferably overnight.
3. Preheat your grill to high heat.
4. Remove the London broil steak from the marinade, allowing any excess marinade to drip off.
5. Place the steak directly on the grill grates and close the lid.
6. Grill the steak for about 5-7 minutes per side, or until it reaches your desired level of doneness.
7. Remove the steak from the grill and let it rest for a few minutes before slicing.

STUFFED PORK CROWN ROAST WITH SAVORY FILLING

Prep Time: 30 minutes | Cook Time: 2 hours | Serving Size: 8 servings

INGREDIENTS

- 1 (10-pound) pork crown roast
- Salt and black pepper
- 2 tbsp olive oil
- Filling: Breadcrumbs, onion, celery, mushrooms, garlic, butter, thyme, sage, salt, black pepper

Cooking times may vary. Use a meat thermometer to ensure proper doneness. The stuffed pork crown roast is a delicious and impressive dish for special occasions. Pair it with your favorite sides for a complete meal.

INSTRUCTIONS

1. Preheat oven to 325°F (163°C).
2. Season pork crown roast with salt and black pepper.
3. Sauté onion, celery, mushrooms, and garlic in olive oil.
4. Add breadcrumbs, butter, thyme, sage, salt, and black pepper to the sautéed vegetables.
5. Stuff the filling into the pork crown roast.
6. Roast in the oven for about 2 hours, until the internal temperature reaches 145°F (63°C).
7. Let the roast rest for 15 minutes before carving.
8. Serve and enjoy!

SWEET HEAT BURNT ENDS

Prep Time: 20 minutes I Cook Time: 5-6 hours I Serving Size: 4-6 servings

INGREDIENTS

- 3 pounds beef chuck roast, cut into 1-inch
- 1/4 cup brown sugar
- 2 tablespoons paprika
- 1 tablespoon chili powder
- 1 tablespoon garlic powder
- 1 tablespoon onion powder
- 1 tablespoon black pepper
- 1 teaspoon salt
- 1/2 teaspoon cayenne pepper
- 1 cup barbecue sauce
- 1/4 cup honey

The combination of sweet and heat in the glaze adds a delicious flavor to the smoky and tender beef cubes.

INSTRUCTIONS

1. Preheat smoker/grill to 250°F (121°C) for indirect heat.
2. Combine brown sugar, paprika, chili powder, garlic powder, onion powder, black pepper, salt, and cayenne pepper for rub.
3. Coat beef chuck cubes with the dry rub.
4. Place seasoned cubes on a wire rack or smoker-safe pan.
5. Smoke cubes for 3-4 hours until mahogany-colored with a firm bark.
6. Mix barbecue sauce, honey, and hot sauce (optional) in a bowl.
7. Transfer beef cubes to a disposable aluminum pan.
8. Pour glaze over cubes, ensuring even coating.
9. Cover pan tightly with foil and return to smoker/grill.
10. Cook cubes for an additional 1-2 hours until tender and caramelized (internal temp: 200°F/93°C).
11. Remove pan from smoker/grill and let burnt ends rest briefly.
12. Serve as appetizer/main course with optional extra sauce.

SAUSAGE BISCUIT SANDWICHES

Prep Time: 10 minutes I Cook Time: 20 minutes I Serving Size: 4 sandwiches

INGREDIENTS

- 8 breakfast sausage patties
- 4 biscuits, split in half
- 4 slices of cheese (cheddar or American)
- 4 large eggs
- Salt and pepper to taste
- Butter or oil for cooking

Feel free to customize the sandwiches by adding condiments like ketchup, mustard, or hot sauce, as well as additional toppings like sliced tomatoes, lettuce, or avocado.

INSTRUCTIONS

1. Preheat a skillet or griddle over medium heat.
2. Cook the breakfast sausage patties according to package instructions until they are browned and cooked through.
3. While the sausages are cooking, toast the split biscuits until golden brown.
4. Remove the sausages from the skillet and set aside.
5. In the same skillet, melt some butter or heat some oil over medium heat.
6. Crack the eggs into the skillet and season with salt and pepper. Cook to your desired level of doneness (e.g., over-easy, sunny-side-up, scrambled).
7. Assemble the sandwiches by placing a slice of cheese on the bottom half of each biscuit.
8. Top with a cooked sausage patty and a cooked egg.
9. Place the top half of the biscuit on top to complete the sandwich.
10. Serve the sausage biscuit sandwiches warm and enjoy!

REVERSE-SEARED FILET MIGNON

Prep Time: 5 minutes | Cook Time: 1 hour | Serving Size: 4 servings

INGREDIENTS

- 4 filet mignon steaks (2 inches thick)
- 1 tablespoon olive oil
- Kosher salt
- Freshly ground black pepper

INSTRUCTIONS

1. Preheat your Traeger grill to 180°F (82°C) or the smoke setting.
2. Brush the steaks with olive oil and season them generously with salt and black pepper.
3. Place the steaks on the grill grate and cook for 45 minutes to 1 hour, or until the internal temperature reaches 120 to 130°F (49-54°C).
4. Remove the steaks from the grill and increase the Traeger's heat to the highest setting.
5. Once preheated, return the steaks to the grill and cook for 1½ to 2½ minutes per side, or until they reach your desired internal temperature.
6. Remove the steaks from the grill and let them rest for a few minutes before serving.

Adjust the cooking time based on your preferred level of doneness using the internal temperature guide provided. The reverse-sear method ensures a tender and evenly cooked filet mignon with a nice crust. Enjoy your perfectly cooked filet mignon!

CHILI-RUBBED GRILLED PORTERHOUSE STEAK

Prep Time: 10 minutes | Cook Time: 10-15 minutes | Serving Size: 2 servings

INGREDIENTS

- 1 porterhouse steak (1.5 to 2 pounds)
- 2 tablespoons chili powder
- 1 tablespoon paprika
- 1 teaspoon garlic powder
- 1 teaspoon onion powder
- 1 teaspoon salt
- 1/2 teaspoon black pepper
- 2 tablespoons olive oil

INSTRUCTIONS

1. In a small bowl, combine the chili powder, paprika, garlic powder, onion powder, salt, and black pepper to create a spice rub.
2. Pat the porterhouse steak dry with a paper towel and brush it with olive oil on both sides.
3. Sprinkle the spice rub evenly over the steak, pressing it gently to adhere to the meat. Let the steak marinate in the refrigerator for 1 hour if desired, or proceed to the next step.
4. Preheat your grill to high heat.
5. Place the porterhouse steak on the hot grill and sear it for 3-4 minutes on each side, or until it develops a charred crust.
6. Reduce the heat to medium and continue cooking the steak for an additional 4-6 minutes per side, or until it reaches your desired level of doneness. Use an instant-read thermometer to check the internal temperature (120°F for rare, 130°F for medium-rare, 140°F for medium).
7. Remove the steak from the grill and let it rest for a few minutes to allow the juices to redistribute.
8. Slice the porterhouse steak against the grain into thick slices.

Pair this flavorful steak with your favorite sides, such as grilled vegetables or roasted potatoes, for a delicious meal.

SMOKED SAUSAGE LASAGNA

Prep Time: 30 minutes | Cook Time: 1 hour | Serving Size: 8-10 servings

INGREDIENTS

- 1 pound smoked sausage, sliced
- 1 onion, chopped
- 2 cloves garlic, minced
- 1 bell pepper, chopped
- 1 can (28 ounces) crushed tomatoes
- 1 can (6 ounces) tomato paste
- 2 teaspoons dried basil
- 1 teaspoon dried oregano
- 1/2 teaspoon salt
- 1/4 teaspoon black pepper
- 3 cups shredded mozzarella cheese
- 1 cup grated Parmesan cheese
- Fresh basil leaves (for garnish)

INSTRUCTIONS

1. Preheat Traeger grill to 375°F (190°C) for indirect cooking.
2. Cook smoked sausage, ground beef, onion, and garlic in a skillet until browned.
3. Add basil, oregano, salt, and pepper. Cook for 2 more minutes.
4. Stir in crushed tomatoes and tomato sauce. Simmer for 10 minutes.
5. Layer cooked lasagna noodles, meat sauce, and cheeses in a greased baking dish.
6. Repeat layers until ingredients are used, ending with a cheese layer on top.
7. Cover dish with foil and place on the grill. Cook for 1 hour.
8. Remove foil and cook for an additional 30 minutes until cheese is golden brown.
9. Let lasagna rest for 10 minutes, garnish with parsley, and serve.

The smoky flavor from the sausage and the slow cooking process on the smoker or grill add a delicious twist to the classic lasagna. Feel free to customize the recipe by adding other ingredients such as spinach, mushrooms, or additional spices. Enjoy this flavorful and comforting smoked sausage lasagna with your family and friends!

BRAISED SHORT RIBS WITH RICH FLAVORS

Prep Time: 20 minutes | Cook Time: 4-5 hours | Serving Size: 4 servings

INGREDIENTS

- 4 lbs beef short ribs
- Salt and pepper
- 2 tbsp vegetable oil
- 1 onion, chopped
- 2 carrots, chopped
- 2 celery stalks, chopped
- 4 cloves garlic, minced
- 2 cups beef broth
- 1 cup red wine
- 2 tbsp tomato paste
- 2 tbsp Worcestershire sauce
- 2 sprigs fresh thyme
- 2 bay leaves
- Chopped fresh parsley (for garnish)

INSTRUCTIONS

1. Season short ribs with salt and pepper. Brown them in a pot with vegetable oil.
2. Sauté chopped onion, carrots, celery, and minced garlic in the pot.
3. Add tomato paste, Worcestershire sauce, and red wine. Simmer for a couple of minutes.
4. Pour in beef broth, add thyme and bay leaves. Return short ribs to the pot.
5. Cover and braise on a Traeger grill at 325°F for 4-5 hours until tender.
6. Skim off excess fat from the sauce.
7. Serve hot, garnished with chopped parsley.
8. Enjoy the rich and tender braised short ribs with your favorite side dishes.

Braising on a Traeger grill infuses the ribs with smoky flavors. Keep an eye on the liquid levels and adjust the temperature as needed. Serve with mashed potatoes or crusty bread to soak up the flavorful sauce.

GRILLED SKIRT STEAK FAJITAS

Prep Time: 15 minutes | Marinating Time: 1-2 hours | Cook Time: 10-15 minutes | Serves 4-6

INGREDIENTS

- 1.5 pounds skirt steak
- 1/4 cup lime juice
- 1/4 cup soy sauce
- 2 tablespoons olive oil
- 2 cloves garlic, minced
- 1 teaspoon chili powder
- 1 teaspoon ground cumin
- 1 teaspoon paprika
- 1/2 teaspoon salt
- 1/4 teaspoon black pepper
- 1 red bell pepper, sliced
- 1 green bell pepper, sliced
- 1 yellow onion, sliced
- Flour tortillas

INSTRUCTIONS

1. Whisk lime juice, soy sauce, olive oil, minced garlic, chili powder, cumin, paprika, salt, and black pepper to create marinade.
2. Marinate skirt steak for 1-2 hours in the fridge.
3. Preheat grill to medium-high heat.
4. Grill steak for 4-6 mins per side, to desired doneness.
5. Let steak rest and slice thinly against the grain.
6. Cook sliced bell peppers and onions until tender and charred.
7. Warm tortillas on grill or stovetop.
8. Assemble fajitas with steak, peppers, and onions on tortillas.
9. Add optional toppings like guacamole, sour cream, salsa, and cilantro.
10. Roll up tortilla and enjoy the grilled skirt steak fajitas.

 Skirt steak is best cooked to medium-rare or medium for optimal tenderness. Adjust the grilling time based on your preference. The marinated steak combined with the flavorful grilled peppers and onions creates a tasty fajita filling. Serve with your favorite side dishes and enjoy this satisfying meal.

SRIRACHA-BOURBON GLAZED SPARE RIBS

Prep Time: 15 minutes | Cook Time: 3-4 hours | Serving Size: 4 servings

INGREDIENTS

- 2 racks of spare ribs
- Salt and pepper to taste
- 1/4 cup sriracha sauce
- 1/4 cup bourbon
- 2 tablespoons soy sauce
- 2 tablespoons honey
- 2 cloves garlic, minced
- 1 teaspoon grated ginger
- Chopped green onions (for garnish)

INSTRUCTIONS

1. Preheat your Traeger grill to 275°F (135°C) and set it up for indirect heat.
2. Season the spare ribs with salt and pepper on both sides.
3. In a small bowl, whisk together sriracha sauce, bourbon, soy sauce, honey, minced garlic, and grated ginger to create the glaze.
4. Place the spare ribs on the grill grate, bone-side down, and close the lid.
5. Smoke the ribs for 2 hours, allowing the flavors to infuse.
6. Brush the glaze generously onto the ribs, coating them evenly.
7. Continue cooking the ribs for an additional 1-2 hours, basting them with the glaze every 30 minutes. The ribs should become tender and caramelized.
8. Remove the spare ribs from the grill and let them rest for a few minutes.
9. Slice the ribs between the bones and garnish with chopped green onions.
10. Serve the Sriracha-Bourbon Glazed Spare Ribs as a delicious and flavorful main dish.

 The combination of sriracha, bourbon, and other savory ingredients creates a sweet and spicy glaze that enhances the smoky flavor of the spare ribs.

LAMB BURGERS WITH BASIL-FETA SAUCE

Prep Time: 15 minutes I Cook Time: 10-12 minutes I Serving Size: 4 servings

INGREDIENTS

- 1 1/2 pounds ground lamb
- 1/4 cup breadcrumbs
- 1/4 cup finely chopped red onion
- 2 cloves garlic, minced
- 1 teaspoon dried oregano
- 1/2 teaspoon ground cumin
- Salt and pepper to taste
- 4 burger buns
- Lettuce leaves, tomato slices, and red onion slices (for garnish)

The combination of flavorful ground lamb, aromatic spices, and the creamy Basil-Feta Sauce creates a mouthwatering burger experience.

INSTRUCTIONS

1. In a mixing bowl, combine ground lamb, breadcrumbs, red onion, minced garlic, dried oregano, ground cumin, salt, and pepper. Mix well until all ingredients are evenly incorporated.
2. Divide the lamb mixture into 4 equal portions and shape them into burger patties.
3. Preheat your grill or stovetop grill pan over medium-high heat.
4. Place the lamb burgers on the grill and cook for 5-6 minutes per side, or until they reach your desired level of doneness.
5. While the burgers are cooking, prepare the Basil-Feta Sauce. In a separate bowl, combine crumbled feta cheese, Greek yogurt, chopped fresh basil, lemon juice, salt, and pepper. Mix well until smooth and creamy.
6. Remove the cooked lamb burgers from the grill and let them rest for a few minutes.
7. Toast the burger buns on the grill for a minute or until lightly browned.
8. Spread a generous amount of the Basil-Feta Sauce on the bottom bun.
9. Place a lamb burger on top of the sauce and garnish with lettuce leaves, tomato slices, and red onion slices.

BBQ SMOKED SALMON

Prep Time: 10 minutes I Cook Time: 1 hour I Serving Size: 4 servings

INGREDIENTS

- 1 pound salmon fillets
- 2 tablespoons olive oil
- 2 tablespoons BBQ seasoning or your favorite dry rub
- Lemon wedges (for serving)

INSTRUCTIONS

1. Preheat your smoker or grill to 225°F (107°C) and set it up for indirect heat.
2. Brush the salmon fillets with olive oil on both sides to prevent sticking.
3. Sprinkle the BBQ seasoning or dry rub evenly over the salmon fillets, coating them well.
4. Place the seasoned salmon fillets directly on the smoker grates or a grilling plank if preferred.
5. Close the lid of the smoker or grill and smoke the salmon for approximately 1 hour, or until the internal temperature reaches 145°F (63°C). The salmon should be opaque and flake easily with a fork.
6. Remove the smoked salmon from the smoker or grill and let it rest for a few minutes.
7. Serve the BBQ smoked salmon with lemon wedges on the side for a burst of freshness and tang.

Smoking the salmon infuses it with a delicious smoky flavor and creates a tender and flaky texture. Make sure to monitor the internal temperature to prevent overcooking.

— CHAPTER 3 —

POULTRY

BUFFALO WINGS RECIPE WITH SPICY TANG

Prep Time: 10 minutes I Cook Time: 45 minutes I Serving Size: 4 servings

INGREDIENTS

- 2 pounds chicken wings
- 1/2 cup all-purpose flour
- 1 teaspoon salt
- 1 teaspoon paprika
- 1/2 teaspoon garlic powder
- 1/2 teaspoon onion powder
- 1/4 teaspoon cayenne pepper
- 1/4 cup unsalted butter, melted
- 1/4 cup hot sauce (Frank's RedHot)

You can adjust the level of spiciness by adding more or less cayenne pepper to the flour mixture or hot sauce. Make sure to monitor the wings closely during the final grilling stage to prevent burning.

INSTRUCTIONS

1. Preheat Traeger grill to 450°F (232°C) for direct heat and set up.
2. In a large bowl, combine flour, salt, paprika, garlic powder, onion powder, and cayenne pepper.
3. Pat dry chicken wings, then coat them evenly with the flour mixture.
4. Arrange wings on the grill grate, ensuring they don't touch. Close lid and cook for 25 minutes until golden brown and crispy.
5. Heat melted butter and hot sauce in a saucepan over low heat.
6. Transfer cooked wings to a mixing bowl, pour hot sauce mixture over them, and toss to coat evenly.
7. Return sauced wings to the grill grate and cook for 5-10 minutes until sauce caramelizes.
8. Remove wings from grill, let them rest briefly, and serve with ranch or blue cheese dressing and celery sticks.

CLASSIC BARBECUE CHICKEN WITH TRADITIONAL FLAVORS

Prep Time: 10 minutes I Cook Time: 1 hour I Serving Size: 4 servings

INGREDIENTS

- 4 chicken leg quarters (or a combination of chicken pieces)
- Salt and pepper to taste
- 1 cup barbecue sauce (your favorite brand or homemade)
- 2 tablespoons olive oil
- 1 tablespoon paprika
- 1 tablespoon brown sugar
- 1 teaspoon garlic powder
- 1 teaspoon onion powder

You can adjust the level of spiciness by adding more or less cayenne pepper to the spice rub.

INSTRUCTIONS

1. Preheat Traeger grill to 350°F (175°C) for indirect heat.
2. Season chicken leg quarters with salt and pepper on both sides.
3. In a small bowl, combine olive oil, paprika, brown sugar, garlic powder, onion powder, and cayenne pepper (if using) to create a spice rub.
4. Generously rub spice mixture all over chicken leg quarters to coat well.
5. Place seasoned chicken leg quarters on grill grate, skin side up, away from direct heat.
6. Close lid and cook for 45 minutes to 1 hour until internal temperature reaches 165°F (74°C) with a meat thermometer.
7. During the last 10 minutes of cooking, brush chicken leg quarters with barbecue sauce, turning to coat both sides. Repeat brushing process until chicken is cooked through and glazed.
8. Remove chicken from grill and let it rest for a few minutes before serving.
9. Garnish with fresh parsley or cilantro, if desired.
10. Serve barbecue chicken with additional barbecue sauce and favorite side dishes.

SMOKED CHICKEN SALAD WITH TASTY DRESSING

Prep Time: 15 minutes I Cook Time: 1 hour I Serving Size: 4 servings

INGREDIENTS

- 2 bone-in chicken breasts, smoked and shredded
- 4 cups mixed salad greens
- 1 cup cherry tomatoes, halved
- 1/2 cup cucumber, diced
- 1/4 cup red onion, thinly sliced
- 1/4 cup sliced almonds, toasted
- 1/4 cup crumbled feta cheese

 The smoked chicken adds a delicious smoky flavor to the salad, but you can also use grilled or roasted chicken if desired.

INSTRUCTIONS

1. Preheat your Traeger grill to 225°F (107°C) and set it up for smoking.
2. Season the chicken breasts with salt and pepper. Place them on the grill grate and smoke for 1 hour, or until the internal temperature reaches 165°F (74°C). Remove the chicken from the grill and let it cool slightly.
3. Once cooled, shred the smoked chicken breasts using two forks or your hands. Set aside.
4. In a large mixing bowl, combine the salad greens, cherry tomatoes, cucumber, red onion, toasted almonds, and crumbled feta cheese.
5. In a separate smaller bowl, whisk together the mayonnaise, Greek yogurt, Dijon mustard, honey, apple cider vinegar, lemon juice, salt, and pepper. Adjust the seasoning to your taste.
6. Pour the dressing over the salad greens and toss until well coated.
7. Add the shredded smoked chicken to the salad and gently toss to combine, ensuring the chicken is evenly distributed.
8. Divide the smoked chicken salad into individual serving plates or bowls.

APPLEWOOD-SMOKED WHOLE TURKEY WITH SMOKY GOODNESS

Prep Time: 30 minutes I Cook Time: 4-5 hours I Serving Size: 8-10 servings

INGREDIENTS

- 1 whole turkey (12-14 pounds)
- 1/2 cup unsalted butter, softened
- 2 tablespoons olive oil
- 2 tablespoons smoked paprika
- 2 tablespoons brown sugar
- 2 teaspoons salt
- 1 teaspoon black pepper
- 1 teaspoon garlic powder
- 1 teaspoon onion powder
- 1 teaspoon dried thyme
- 1 teaspoon dried rosemary
- 2 cups applewood smoking pellets/chips
- Applewood chunks for smoking

INSTRUCTIONS

1. Preheat Traeger grill to 275°F (135°C) for indirect heat smoking.
2. Rinse and pat dry the turkey.
3. Mix butter, olive oil, spices to form a paste.
4. Loosen turkey skin and rub butter mixture under it.
5. Place turkey on rack in roasting pan or directly on grill grate.
6. Fill smoker box with applewood pellets/chips.
7. Insert meat thermometer into thigh.
8. Smoke turkey for 4-5 hours at consistent temperature, adding applewood as needed.
9. Remove turkey at 165°F (74°C) internal temperature and let it rest.
10. Carve and serve smoked turkey as centerpiece.

 The applewood smoke adds a delicious smoky flavor to the turkey, enhancing its natural juiciness. Make sure to monitor the internal temperature of the turkey using a meat thermometer to ensure it reaches the recommended safe temperature. Adjust the cooking time accordingly based on the size of your turkey. Enjoy the smoky goodness of this applewood-smoked whole turkey with your favorite sides and sauces.

SMOKED DRUMSTICKS WITH FLAVORFUL TWIST

Prep Time: 15 minutes I Cook Time: 2-3 hours I Serving Size: 4 servings

INGREDIENTS

- 8 chicken drumsticks
- 2 tablespoons olive oil
- 2 tablespoons soy sauce
- 2 tablespoons honey
- 2 tablespoons Dijon mustard
- 1 tablespoon smoked paprika
- 1 teaspoon garlic powder
- 1 teaspoon onion powder
- 1 teaspoon dried oregano
- 1/2 teaspoon salt
- 1/2 teaspoon black pepper
- Applewood smoking pellets/chips

INSTRUCTIONS

1. Preheat Traeger grill to 275°F (135°C) for indirect heat smoking.
2. Whisk together olive oil, soy sauce, honey, mustard, spices to make marinade.
3. Place chicken drumsticks in marinade for at least 30 minutes.
4. Fill smoker box with applewood pellets/chips.
5. Arrange drumsticks on grill grate, spaced apart.
6. Smoke drumsticks for 2-3 hours, basting every 30 minutes.
7. Remove drumsticks and let them rest.
8. Serve with desired sauces and sides.

 The smoky flavor from the Traeger grill adds a delicious twist to these drumsticks. Feel free to adjust the amount of seasoning and spices according to your taste preferences. Serve the drumsticks as a main course or as a finger-licking appetizer at your next barbecue or gathering. Enjoy the flavorful twist of these smoked drumsticks!

SMOKED PHEASANT RECIPE WITH DISTINCTIVE TASTE

Prep Time: 20 minutes I Cook Time: 2-3 hours I Serving Size: 4 servings

INGREDIENTS

- 2 pheasant breasts
- 2 tablespoons olive oil
- 2 tablespoons soy sauce
- 2 tablespoons maple syrup
- 1 tablespoon Dijon mustard
- 1 teaspoon garlic powder
- 1 teaspoon smoked paprika
- 1/2 teaspoon dried thyme
- 1/2 teaspoon salt
- 1/2 teaspoon black pepper
- Applewood smoking pellets/chips

INSTRUCTIONS

1. Preheat Traeger grill to 275°F (135°C) for indirect heat smoking.
2. Whisk together olive oil, soy sauce, maple syrup, mustard, spices to make marinade.
3. Marinate pheasant breasts for at least 15 minutes.
4. Fill smoker box with applewood pellets/chips.
5. Place pheasant breasts on grill grate.
6. Smoke for 2-3 hours until internal temperature reaches 165°F (74°C), basting with marinade.
7. Remove from grill and let them rest.
8. Slice and serve as a main course or in salads, sandwiches, or wraps.

 Pheasant has a unique and rich flavor that pairs wonderfully with the smoky essence from the Traeger grill. Feel free to adjust the seasonings and marinade ingredients according to your taste preferences. Enjoy the distinctive taste of this smoked pheasant recipe and impress your guests with this flavorful dish!

SMOKED CHICKEN CORN CHOWDER WITH RICH FLAVORS

Prep Time: 20 minutes I Cook Time: 45 minutes I Serving Size: 4 servings

INGREDIENTS

- 2 cups smoked chicken, shredded or diced
- 2 tablespoons butter
- 1 onion, diced
- 2 cloves garlic, minced
- 2 cups frozen corn kernels
- 2 medium potatoes, peeled and diced
- 4 cups chicken broth
- 1 cup heavy cream
- 1 teaspoon dried thyme
- 1 teaspoon smoked paprika
- Salt and pepper to taste
- Chopped fresh parsley (for garnish)

INSTRUCTIONS

1. Melt butter, sauté onion and garlic until fragrant.
2. Add corn and potatoes, cook briefly.
3. Pour in chicken broth, simmer until potatoes are tender.
4. Blend half of the soup for thickness, keeping some texture.
5. Stir in smoked chicken, thyme, paprika, salt, and pepper. Simmer for 10 minutes.
6. Pour in heavy cream, simmer until heated through.
7. Let the chowder rest.
8. Ladle into bowls, garnish with parsley.
9. Serve hot and enjoy the flavorful smoked chicken corn chowder.

The smoky flavor of the chicken adds a delicious depth to this corn chowder. Feel free to adjust the seasonings according to your taste preferences. You can also add additional ingredients such as diced carrots or bell peppers for extra flavor and texture. This hearty and flavorful smoked chicken corn chowder is perfect for cozy meals on cold days.

TERIYAKI TURKEY BREAST TENDERLOIN FOR ASIAN-INSPIRED DELIGHT

Prep Time: 10 minutes I Marinating Time: 1 hour I Cook Time: 25 minutes I Serves 4

INGREDIENTS

- 1.5 pounds turkey breast tenderloin
- 1/4 cup soy sauce
- 2 tablespoons honey
- 2 tablespoons rice vinegar
- 2 tablespoons sesame oil
- 2 cloves garlic, minced
- 1 teaspoon grated ginger
- 1 tablespoon cornstarch
- 2 tablespoons water
- Toasted sesame seeds (for garnish)
- Sliced green onions (for garnish)

INSTRUCTIONS

1. Whisk together soy sauce, honey, vinegar, sesame oil, garlic, and ginger for marinade.
2. Coat turkey tenderloin with marinade, refrigerate for 1 hour.
3. Preheat Traeger grill to medium-high heat (around 400°F).
4. Grill turkey for 20-25 minutes until internal temperature reaches 165°F.
5. Prepare teriyaki glaze by dissolving cornstarch in water, then simmering with remaining marinade.
6. Brush turkey with teriyaki glaze, let it rest.
7. Slice turkey and garnish with sesame seeds and green onions.
8. Serve hot with rice or vegetables for an Asian-inspired meal.

You can adjust the sweetness or saltiness of the teriyaki marinade by adding more honey or soy sauce, respectively. If you prefer a milder garlic and ginger flavor, you can reduce the amount according to your taste. Enjoy the tender and flavorful teriyaki turkey breast tenderloin, a delightful dish with an Asian twist.

HONEY-SRIRACHA CHICKEN BREAST WITH SWEET & SPICY BLEND

Prep Time: 10 minutes I Marinating Time: 30 mins I Cook Time: 20 minutes I Serves 4

INGREDIENTS

- 4 boneless, skinless chicken breasts
- 1/4 cup honey
- 2 tablespoons sriracha sauce
- 2 tablespoons soy sauce
- 2 cloves garlic, minced
- 1 tablespoon lime juice
- 1 tablespoon vegetable oil
- Salt and pepper to taste
- Chopped fresh cilantro (for garnish)
- Lime wedges (for serving)

INSTRUCTIONS

1. Whisk honey, sriracha, soy sauce, garlic, lime juice, oil, salt, and pepper for marinade.
2. Marinate chicken in mixture for 30 minutes.
3. Preheat Traeger grill to medium-high heat (around 400°F).
4. Grill chicken, basting with marinade, until internal temperature reaches 165°F.
5. Let chicken rest and slice as desired.
6. Garnish with cilantro and serve with lime wedges.
7. Enjoy the sweet and spicy honey-sriracha chicken with your preferred side dishes.

 Adjust the amount of sriracha sauce according to your desired level of spiciness. You can also add more honey for a sweeter taste or additional lime juice for extra tanginess. Remember to baste the chicken with the marinade during grilling to enhance the flavor.

WILD WEST WINGS RECIPE WITH BOLD FLAVORS

Prep Time: 15 minutes I Marinating Time: 1 hour I Cook Time: 25 minutes I Serves 4

INGREDIENTS

- 2 pounds chicken wings
- 1/4 cup barbecue sauce
- 2 tablespoons Worcestershire sauce
- 2 tablespoons hot sauce
- 2 tablespoons brown sugar
- 1 tablespoon smoked paprika
- 1 teaspoon garlic powder
- 1 teaspoon onion powder
- 1 teaspoon salt
- 1/2 teaspoon black pepper
- Vegetable oil (for grilling)
- Chopped fresh cilantro (for garnish)
- Lime wedges (for serving)

INSTRUCTIONS

1. Combine barbecue sauce, Worcestershire sauce, hot sauce, brown sugar, paprika, garlic powder, onion powder, salt, and pepper for marinade.
2. Marinate chicken wings for at least 1 hour.
3. Preheat Traeger grill to medium-high heat and grease grill grates.
4. Grill wings, basting with marinade, until cooked through and crispy.
5. Sprinkle with cilantro and serve with lime wedges.
6. Enjoy the flavorful Wild West wings as an appetizer or main dish with your favorite dipping sauce.

 Adjust the amount of hot sauce used according to your desired level of spiciness. You can also customize the flavor by adding additional spices or seasonings. The longer you marinate the wings, the more intense the flavors will be. Remember to baste the wings during grilling to keep them moist and enhance the taste.

MANDARIN-GLAZED DUCK COOKING RECIPE

Prep Time: 20 minutes | Marinating Time: 2 hours | Cook Time: 1 hour | Serves 4

INGREDIENTS

- 4 duck breasts
- Salt and pepper to taste
- 1 cup mandarin orange juice
- 1/4 cup soy sauce
- 1/4 cup honey
- 2 tablespoons rice vinegar
- 2 tablespoons cornstarch
- 1 tablespoon grated fresh ginger
- 2 cloves garlic, minced
- Sesame seeds (for garnish)
- Sliced green onions (for garnish)

INSTRUCTIONS

1. ChatGPT
2. Season duck breasts with salt and pepper.
3. Combine mandarin orange juice, soy sauce, honey, rice vinegar, cornstarch, ginger, and garlic to make the marinade.
4. Marinate duck breasts for at least 2 hours.
5. Preheat Traeger grill to medium-high heat.
6. Grill duck breasts skin-side down until crispy and browned.
7. Flip and brush with reserved marinade.
8. Continue grilling until desired internal temperature is reached.
9. Let the duck breasts rest and slice them diagonally.
10. Drizzle with remaining marinade and garnish with sesame seeds and green onions.
11. Serve the Mandarin-Glazed Duck hot with rice or side dishes.

 Adjust the cooking time according to the thickness of the duck breasts and your desired level of doneness. You can use a meat thermometer to ensure the duck is cooked to your preferred temperature.

SMOKED CHICKEN QUARTERS WITH TENDER RESULTS

Prep Time: 10 minutes | Marinating Time: 2 hours | Cook Time: 2-3 hours | Serves 4

INGREDIENTS

- 4 chicken leg quarters
- Salt and pepper to taste
- 2 tablespoons olive oil
- 2 tablespoons paprika
- 1 tablespoon garlic powder
- 1 tablespoon onion powder
- 1 tablespoon dried thyme
- 1 tablespoon dried oregano
- BBQ sauce (optional, for serving)

INSTRUCTIONS

1. Preheat Traeger grill to 225°F (107°C).
2. Season chicken leg quarters with salt and pepper.
3. Rub with spice paste (olive oil, paprika, garlic powder, onion powder, dried thyme, dried oregano).
4. Smoke for 2-3 hours until internal temperature reaches 165°F (74°C).
5. Optional: Brush with BBQ sauce during last 15 minutes.
6. Let rest and serve hot with desired sides.

 Cooking time may vary depending on the size and thickness of the chicken leg quarters. It's essential to ensure the chicken reaches an internal temperature of 165°F (74°C) for safe consumption. The low and slow smoking process will result in tender and flavorful chicken with a smoky aroma. Enjoy the juicy and delicious smoked chicken quarters straight from your Traeger grill.

LEMONADE CHICKEN DRUMSTICKS WITH ZESTY FLAVOR

Prep Time: 10 minutes | Marinating Time: 1 hour | Cook Time: 35-40 minutes | Serves 4

INGREDIENTS

- 8 chicken drumsticks
- 1 cup lemonade
- 1/4 cup soy sauce
- 2 tablespoons honey
- 2 tablespoons olive oil
- 2 cloves garlic, minced
- 1 teaspoon lemon zest
- 1/2 teaspoon black pepper
- 1/2 teaspoon salt
- Fresh parsley, for garnish (optional)

INSTRUCTIONS

1. Combine lemonade, soy sauce, honey, olive oil, minced garlic, lemon zest, black pepper, and salt.
2. Marinate drumsticks for at least 1 hour or overnight.
3. Preheat Traeger grill to 375°F (190°C) for direct heat.
4. Grill drumsticks for 35-40 minutes, flipping halfway, until internal temperature reaches 165°F (74°C).
5. Let rest and garnish with fresh parsley.
6. Serve hot with desired sides.

Adjust the cooking time based on the thickness of the drumsticks. The marinade adds a tangy and zesty flavor to the chicken, making it juicy and delicious. Enjoy these lemonade chicken drumsticks straight from your Traeger grill.

EASY RAPID-FIRE ROAST CHICKEN FOR QUICK PREPARATION

Prep Time: 10 minutes | Cook Time: 45-55 minutes | Serving Size: 4 servings

INGREDIENTS

- 1 whole chicken (3-4 pounds)
- 2 tablespoons olive oil
- 1 tablespoon paprika
- 1 teaspoon garlic powder
- 1 teaspoon onion powder
- 1 teaspoon dried thyme
- 1 teaspoon dried rosemary
- 1 teaspoon salt
- 1/2 teaspoon black pepper

INSTRUCTIONS

1. Preheat your Traeger grill to 450°F (230°C) and set it up for indirect heat.
2. Rinse the chicken inside and out with cold water and pat it dry with paper towels.
3. In a small bowl, mix together the olive oil, paprika, garlic powder, onion powder, dried thyme, dried rosemary, salt, and black pepper to create a spice rub.
4. Rub the spice mixture all over the chicken, making sure to coat it evenly.
5. Place the seasoned chicken directly on the grill grate, breast-side up.
6. Close the lid of the Traeger grill and roast the chicken for 45-55 minutes, or until the internal temperature reaches 165°F (74°C) when measured with a meat thermometer. The high heat will help crisp up the skin while keeping the meat juicy and flavorful.
7. Once the chicken is cooked through and golden brown, remove it from the grill and let it rest for 10 minutes before carving.
8. Carve the roasted chicken into serving pieces and serve hot. It pairs well with roasted vegetables, mashed potatoes, or a fresh green salad.

This rapid-fire roast chicken method is perfect for when you need a quick and delicious meal.

SMOKED TURKEY BREAST WITH SAVORY GOODNESS

Prep Time: 15 minutes I Cook Time: 3-4 hours I Serving Size: 6-8 servings

INGREDIENTS

- 1 turkey breast (4-5 pounds)

- 2 tablespoons olive oil

- 2 teaspoons dried thyme

- 2 teaspoons dried rosemary

- 2 teaspoons paprika

- 2 teaspoons garlic powder

- 1 teaspoon salt

- 1/2 teaspoon black pepper

- Wood pellets of your choice (such as hickory or apple)

Smoking the turkey breast on a Traeger grill imparts a delicious smoky flavor and helps to keep the meat tender and juicy.

INSTRUCTIONS

1. Preheat Traeger grill to 225°F (107°C) for indirect heat.
2. Rinse and dry turkey breast.
3. In a small bowl, combine the dried thyme, dried rosemary, paprika, garlic powder, salt, and black pepper to create a savory spice rub.
4. Brush turkey breast with olive oil.
5. Sprinkle the spice rub over the turkey breast, gently pressing it into the surface to adhere.
6. Place turkey breast on grill grate away from direct heat.
7. Add wood pellets to your Traeger grill according to the manufacturer's instructions, selecting a flavor that complements the turkey.
8. Smoke turkey for 3-4 hours until internal temperature reaches 165°F (74°C).
9. Check the temperature in the thickest part of the turkey breast without touching the bone.
10. Slice and serve with desired accompaniments.

SMO–FRIED CHICKEN RECIPE WITH SMOKY GOODNESS

Prep Time: 15 minutes I Cook Time: 30-35 minutes I Serving Size: 4 servings

INGREDIENTS

- 4 chicken drumsticks

- 4 chicken thighs

- 1 cup buttermilk

- 1 cup all-purpose flour

- 1 teaspoon smoked paprika

- 1 teaspoon garlic powder

- 1 teaspoon onion powder

- 1 teaspoon salt

- 1/2 teaspoon black pepper

- Vegetable oil, for frying

Smo-fried chicken combines the crispy texture of traditional fried chicken with the smoky flavor of a Traeger grill.

INSTRUCTIONS

1. Marinate chicken in buttermilk for at least 1 hour, preferably overnight.
2. Mix flour, paprika, garlic powder, onion powder, salt, and pepper in a shallow dish.
3. Coat chicken in flour mixture, pressing firmly.
4. Heat vegetable oil in a deep skillet or frying pan over medium heat. The oil should be about 1 inch deep.
5. Fry chicken for 15-18 minutes per side until golden brown and cooked through.
6. As the chicken cooks, adjust the heat if necessary to maintain a steady temperature and prevent burning.
7. Once the chicken is cooked, remove it from the skillet and place it on a paper towel-lined plate to drain excess oil.
8. Let the chicken rest for a few minutes before serving. This will help to retain its juiciness.
9. Serve the smo-fried chicken hot with your favorite sides such as mashed potatoes, coleslaw, or cornbread.

CORNISH GAME HEN WITH FLAVORFUL TWIST

Prep Time: 10 minutes I Cook Time: 50-60 minutes I Serving Size: 2 servings

INGREDIENTS

- 2 Cornish game hens
- 2 tablespoons olive oil
- 2 cloves garlic, minced
- 1 teaspoon dried thyme
- 1 teaspoon paprika
- 1/2 teaspoon salt
- 1/4 teaspoon black pepper
- 1 lemon, sliced
- Fresh parsley, for garnish

This Cornish game hen recipe offers a flavorful twist with the combination of garlic, thyme, and lemon.

INSTRUCTIONS

1. Preheat your Traeger grill to 375°F (190°C).
2. Pat the Cornish game hens dry with paper towels. This will help to achieve crispy skin.
3. In a small bowl, combine the olive oil, minced garlic, dried thyme, paprika, salt, and black pepper. Mix well to create a flavorful marinade.
4. Rub the marinade all over the Cornish game hens, ensuring they are well coated.
5. Place the lemon slices inside the cavity of each Cornish game hen. This will infuse the meat with a citrusy aroma.
6. Place the game hens directly on the grill grate, breast-side up.
7. Close the lid of the grill and cook the hens for 50-60 minutes, or until the internal temperature reaches 165°F (74°C) when measured with a meat thermometer. The skin should be golden brown and crispy.
8. Once cooked, remove the Cornish game hens from the grill and let them rest for 5 minutes to allow the juices to redistribute.
9. Garnish with fresh parsley for added freshness and presentation.

SMOKED AIRLINE CHICKEN WITH TENDER

Prep Time: 10 minutes I Cook Time: 1 hour 30 minutes I Serving Size: 2 servings

INGREDIENTS

- 2 airline chicken breasts
- 2 tablespoons olive oil
- 1 tablespoon smoked paprika
- 1 teaspoon garlic powder
- 1 teaspoon onion powder
- 1 teaspoon dried thyme
- 1 teaspoon salt
- 1/2 teaspoon black pepper
- Wood pellets of your choice

Airline chicken breasts are bone-in and skin-on, which helps retain moisture and flavor during the smoking process.

INSTRUCTIONS

1. Preheat your Traeger grill to 225°F (107°C) and ensure it is set up for indirect grilling.
2. Pat dry the airline chicken breasts with paper towels to remove any excess moisture.
3. In a small bowl, combine the olive oil, smoked paprika, garlic powder, onion powder, dried thyme, salt, and black pepper. Mix well to create a flavorful rub.
4. Rub the spice mixture evenly over both sides of the chicken breasts, ensuring they are well coated.
5. Place the chicken breasts directly on the grill grate, skin-side up.
6. Insert a meat thermometer into the thickest part of one chicken breast, avoiding contact with the bone.
7. Close the lid of the grill and smoke the chicken breasts at 225°F (107°C) for approximately 1 hour 30 minutes, or until the internal temperature reaches 165°F (74°C). The low and slow cooking process will result in tender and juicy chicken with a smoky flavor.
8. Once the chicken breasts reach the desired temperature, let them rest for 5 minutes before serving.

SMOKED WHOLE CHICKEN WITH DELICIOUS SEASONINGS

Prep Time: 15 minutes | Cook Time: 3 hours | Serving Size: 4 servings

INGREDIENTS

- 1 whole chicken (4-5 pounds)
- 2 tablespoons olive oil
- 2 teaspoons smoked paprika
- 2 teaspoons garlic powder
- 1 teaspoon dried thyme
- 1 teaspoon dried rosemary
- 1 teaspoon salt
- 1/2 teaspoon black pepper
- Wood pellets of your choice

This Cornish game hen recipe offers a flavorful twist with the combination of garlic, thyme, and lemon.

INSTRUCTIONS

1. Preheat your Traeger grill to 225°F (107°C) and set it up for indirect grilling.
2. Rinse the whole chicken under cold water and pat it dry with paper towels.
3. In a small bowl, combine the olive oil, smoked paprika, garlic powder, dried thyme, dried rosemary, salt, and black pepper. Mix well to create a flavorful rub.
4. Rub the spice mixture evenly over the entire surface of the chicken, including the cavity. Make sure to get under the skin as well for maximum flavor.
5. Place the seasoned chicken directly on the grill grate, breast-side up.
6. Insert a meat thermometer into the thickest part of the chicken, without touching the bone.
7. Close the grill lid and smoke the chicken at 225°F (107°C) for about 3 hours, or until the internal temperature reaches 165°F (74°C).
8. Rest the chicken for 10-15 minutes before carving to allow the juices to redistribute and ensure maximum juiciness.
9. Carve the smoked whole chicken into serving pieces, such as drumsticks, thighs, wings, and breast meat.

ROASTED WHOLE CHICKEN WITH CLASSIC PREPARATION

Prep Time: 15 minutes | Cook Time: 1 hour 30 minutes | Serving Size: 4 servings

INGREDIENTS

- 1 whole chicken (4-5 pounds)
- 2 tablespoons butter, softened
- 2 cloves garlic, minced
- 1 teaspoon dried thyme
- 1 teaspoon dried rosemary
- 1 teaspoon paprika
- Salt and pepper to taste
- 1 lemon, halved
- Fresh herbs

Roasting a whole chicken on a Traeger grill with classic preparation results in tender, juicy meat with a hint of smoky flavor. The herb butter and aromatic lemon infuse the chicken with wonderful flavors.

INSTRUCTIONS

1. Preheat grill to 375°F (190°C) for indirect grilling.
2. Rinse and dry chicken.
3. Mix softened butter, garlic, herbs, paprika, salt, and pepper.
4. Spread herb butter under chicken skin.
5. Season outside with salt and pepper.
6. Fill cavity with lemon and herbs, tie legs.
7. Grill chicken breast-side up for 1 hour 30 minutes or until internal temperature is 165°F (74°C).
8. Let chicken rest for 10-15 minutes.
9. Carve and serve with sides like roasted vegetables or mashed potatoes.

PICKLE-BRINED CHICKEN THIGHS FOR TANGY TWIST

Prep Time: 10 minutes | Brining Time: 2 hours | Cook Time: 30 minutes | Serves 4

INGREDIENTS

- 8 bone-in, skin-on chicken thighs
- 2 cups pickle juice
- 1 tablespoon olive oil
- 1 teaspoon paprika
- 1/2 teaspoon garlic powder
- 1/2 teaspoon onion powder
- Salt and pepper to taste
- Chopped fresh dill for garnish

INSTRUCTIONS

1. Preheat grill to 375°F (190°C) for indirect grilling.
2. Rinse and dry chicken.
3. Mix softened butter, garlic, herbs, paprika, salt, and pepper.
4. Spread herb butter under chicken skin.
5. Season outside with salt and pepper.
6. Fill cavity with lemon and herbs, tie legs.
7. Grill chicken breast-side up for 1 hour 30 minutes or until internal temperature is 165°F (74°C).
8. Let chicken rest for 10-15 minutes.
9. Carve and serve with sides like roasted vegetables or mashed potatoes.

The pickle brine adds a tangy and unique flavor to the chicken thighs while also keeping them juicy and tender. The Traeger grill infuses a subtle smoky element into the dish, further enhancing the overall taste.

SMOKED TURKEY WINGS WITH SMOKY AROMAS

Prep Time: 10 minutes | Marinating Time: 2 hours | Cook Time: 3-4 hours | Serves 4

INGREDIENTS

- 4 turkey wings
- 1/4 cup olive oil
- 2 tablespoons Worcestershire sauce
- 2 tablespoons soy sauce
- 2 tablespoons apple cider vinegar
- 1 tablespoon brown sugar
- 1 tablespoon smoked paprika
- 1 teaspoon garlic powder
- 1 teaspoon onion powder
- 1/2 teaspoon black pepper
- 1/2 teaspoon salt
- Wood pellets for smoking

INSTRUCTIONS

1. Whisk together olive oil, Worcestershire sauce, soy sauce, apple cider vinegar, brown sugar, smoked paprika, garlic powder, onion powder, black pepper, and salt for marinade.
2. Marinate turkey wings for at least 2 hours.
3. Preheat Traeger grill to 225°F (107°C) for indirect smoking.
4. Drain marinade from wings.
5. Add wood pellets to grill.
6. Place turkey wings on grill grate, avoiding touching.
7. Smoke wings for 3-4 hours until internal temperature reaches 165°F (74°C).
8. Rotate wings for even smoking.
9. Let wings rest before serving.
10. Serve smoked turkey wings as appetizers or main course with sauces or dips.

The low and slow smoking process infuses the turkey wings with smoky aromas, creating a flavorful and tender meat.

SMOKED CHICKEN ENCHILADAS FOR CINCO DE MAYO CELEBRATION

Prep Time: 20 minutes I Cook Time: 45 minutes I Serving Size: 4 servings

INGREDIENTS

- 2 cups smoked chicken, shredded
- 8 small flour tortillas
- 1 cup enchilada sauce
- 1 cup shredded cheese
- 1/2 cup diced onions
- 1/2 cup diced bell peppers
- 1/4 cup chopped fresh cilantro
- 1 tablespoon olive oil
- 1 teaspoon ground cumin
- 1 teaspoon chili powder
- Salt and pepper to taste

You can adjust the spice level by adding more or less chili powder and jalapeños according to your preference.

INSTRUCTIONS

1. Preheat your Traeger grill to 350°F (175°C) and set it up for indirect grilling.
2. In a skillet, sauté diced onions and bell peppers in olive oil until softened.
3. Add shredded chicken, spices, and cook briefly.
4. Warm flour tortillas on the grill to make them pliable.
5. Spread a spoonful of enchilada sauce on the bottom of a baking dish.
6. Fill each tortilla with the chicken mixture, roll it up tightly, and place it seam-side down in the baking dish. Repeat with the remaining tortillas.
7. Pour sauce over enchiladas.
8. Sprinkle shredded cheese over the top of the enchiladas.
9. Place the baking dish on the Traeger grill and cook for 30-35 minutes, or until the cheese is melted and bubbly.
10. Remove the enchiladas from the grill and let them cool slightly.
11. Garnish with chopped fresh cilantro and serve hot.
12. Serve with your favorite toppings such as sour cream, sliced avocado, chopped tomatoes, chopped green onions, and sliced jalapeños.

APPLE AND SAGE STUFFED QUAIL RECIPE

Prep Time: 30 minutes I Cook Time: 25 minutes I Serving Size: 2 servings

INGREDIENTS

- 2 quails, whole
- 1 apple, peeled and diced
- 1/4 cup breadcrumbs
- 2 tablespoons chopped fresh sage
- 2 tablespoons chopped shallots
- 2 tablespoons unsalted butter, melted
- Salt and pepper to taste
- Kitchen twine for trussing

The Traeger grill adds a delicious smoky flavor to the quails, enhancing the overall taste of the dish. The combination of sweet apple, fragrant sage, and tender quail meat creates a mouthwatering experience.

INSTRUCTIONS

1. Preheat your Traeger grill to 400°F (200°C) for direct grilling.
2. In a bowl, mix diced apple, breadcrumbs, chopped sage, chopped shallots, melted butter, salt, and pepper.
3. Fill the quail cavities with the apple and sage stuffing, being careful not to overstuff.
4. Truss the quails with kitchen twine to hold their shape.
5. Season the outside of the quails with salt and pepper.
6. Place the quails on the grill grate, breast side up.
7. Grill for 20-25 minutes until the internal temperature reaches 165°F (74°C) and the skin is crispy.
8. Remove the quails from the grill and let them rest.
9. Remove the twine and serve the quails whole or halved.
10. Garnish with fresh sage leaves, if desired.
11. Enjoy the delicious apple and sage stuffed quails with your favorite sides.

BUTTERED THANKSGIVING TURKEY WITH CLASSIC FLAVORS

Prep Time: 30 minutes | Cook Time: Varies based on turkey size | Serving Size: 4-6 servings

INGREDIENTS

- 1 whole turkey
- Salt and pepper to taste
- 1 cup unsalted butter, softened
- 2 tablespoons chopped fresh herbs
- 4 garlic cloves, minced
- 1 lemon, sliced
- 1 onion, quartered
- 4 cups turkey or chicken broth

Cooking times can vary based on the size and type of turkey, so it's essential to use a meat thermometer to ensure it is cooked to the proper internal temperature.

INSTRUCTIONS

1. Preheat Traeger grill to 325°F (163°C) for indirect heat.
2. Pat the turkey dry with paper towels.
3. Season the turkey with salt and pepper.
4. Mix softened butter, fresh herbs, and minced garlic to create herb butter.
5. Gently loosen the turkey skin and spread herb butter underneath.
6. Place lemon slices and onion quarters inside the cavity.
7. Tie the turkey's legs together with kitchen twine.
8. Place the turkey on a roasting rack or grill grate, breast side up.
9. Pour broth into a drip pan or roasting pan underneath.
10. Insert a meat thermometer into the thigh without touching the bone.
11. Roast the turkey until the internal temperature reaches 165°F (74°C).
12. Baste the turkey with pan juices every 30 minutes.
13. Remove the turkey from the grill and let it rest for 20-30 minutes.
14. Carve the turkey and arrange slices on a platter.
15. Garnish with fresh herbs, if desired.
16. Serve with traditional Thanksgiving sides.

SMOKE-ROASTED CHICKEN THIGHS WITH SMOKY INFUSION

Prep Time: 10 minutes | Cook Time: 1 hour | Serving Size: 4 servings

INGREDIENTS

- 8 chicken thighs, bone-in and skin-on
- 2 tablespoons olive oil
- 2 tablespoons smoked paprika
- 1 tablespoon garlic powder
- 1 tablespoon onion powder
- 1 tablespoon brown sugar
- 1 teaspoon salt
- 1 teaspoon black pepper

Adjust the cooking time as needed, depending on the size and thickness of the chicken thighs. The spice rub can be customized to suit your taste preferences by adjusting the amount of cayenne pepper or adding other spices and herbs.

INSTRUCTIONS

1. Preheat Traeger grill to 275°F (135°C) for indirect heat.
2. Combine smoked paprika, garlic powder, onion powder, brown sugar, salt, black pepper, and cayenne pepper (optional) to create a spice rub.
3. Pat chicken thighs dry and drizzle with olive oil, coating them evenly.
4. Generously sprinkle spice rub on both sides of the chicken thighs, pressing it into the skin.
5. Place chicken thighs on the grill grate, skin side up, and close the lid.
6. Smoke-roast for about 1 hour or until internal temperature reaches 165°F (74°C).
7. Remove from the grill and let them rest.
8. Serve the smoke-roasted chicken thighs hot as a main course with your favorite sides.

BUFFALO CHICKEN WRAPS WITH SPICY KICK

Prep Time: 15 minutes | Cook Time: 20 minutes | Serving Size: 4 wraps

INGREDIENTS

- 2 boneless, skinless chicken breasts
- Salt and pepper to taste
- 1/4 cup all-purpose flour
- 1/4 cup hot sauce (such as Frank's RedHot)
- 2 tablespoons unsalted butter, melted
- 4 large tortillas (10-inch diameter)
- 1/2 cup ranch or blue cheese dressing
- 1 cup shredded lettuce
- 1/2 cup diced tomatoes
- 1/4 cup sliced green onions

INSTRUCTIONS

1. Preheat Traeger grill to 400°F (200°C).
2. Season chicken breasts with salt and pepper, dust with flour.
3. Grill chicken for about 10 minutes per side until internal temperature reaches 165°F (74°C). Let it rest.
4. In a bowl, combine hot sauce and melted butter.
5. Shred the cooked chicken and toss in buffalo sauce.
6. Warm tortillas on the grill for 1 minute per side.
7. Spread dressing on each tortilla, leaving a border.
8. Place buffalo chicken in the center of each tortilla.
9. Top with lettuce, tomatoes, and green onions.
10. Fold and roll tightly to form a wrap.
11. Cut wraps in half diagonally and serve immediately.

Adjust the level of spiciness by adding more or less hot sauce to the buffalo sauce mixture.

SPATCHCOCKED TURKEY FOR JUICY AND QUICK COOKING

Prep Time: 15 minutes | Cook Time: 1 hour 30 minutes | Serving Size: 8 servings

INGREDIENTS

- 1 whole turkey (12-14 pounds)
- Salt and pepper to taste
- 2 tablespoons olive oil
- 1 tablespoon dried herbs
- 4 cloves garlic, minced
- 1 lemon, sliced
- 1 onion, quartered

INSTRUCTIONS

1. Preheat your Traeger grill to 400°F (200°C).
2. Place the turkey on a cutting board breast-side down. Using kitchen shears or a sharp knife, cut along one side of the backbone from the tail to the neck. Repeat on the other side to remove the backbone.
3. Flip the turkey over and press down firmly on the breastbone to flatten it. You may hear a cracking sound, which is normal. This is called spatchcocking.
4. Pat the turkey dry with paper towels. Season it generously with salt and pepper on both sides.
5. In a small bowl, combine the olive oil, dried herbs, and minced garlic. Rub this mixture all over the turkey, making sure to get it under the skin as well.
6. Place the lemon slices and quartered onion on the grill grate. Lay the spatchcocked turkey directly on top of the lemon and onion, skin-side up.
7. Close the grill lid and roast the turkey for approximately 1 hour 30 minutes, or until the internal temperature reaches 165°F (74°C) in the thickest part of the breast and thigh.
8. Once cooked, remove the turkey from the grill and let it rest for 15-20 minutes before carving.

Spatchcocking the turkey helps it cook more evenly and quickly, resulting in juicy and flavorful meat.

SKINNY SMOKED CHICKEN BREASTS FOR HEALTHIER OPTION

Prep Time: 10 minutes | Cook Time: 1 hour | Serving Size: 4 servings

INGREDIENTS

- 4 boneless, skinless chicken breasts
- 2 tablespoons olive oil
- 1 tablespoon smoked paprika
- 1 teaspoon garlic powder
- 1 teaspoon onion powder
- 1 teaspoon dried oregano
- 1 teaspoon salt
- 1/2 teaspoon black pepper
- Lemon wedges (for serving)

Smoking chicken breasts adds a delicious smoky flavor while keeping them lean and healthy. The spice rub adds a burst of flavor without adding excess calories or fat.

INSTRUCTIONS

1. Preheat your Traeger grill to 225°F (107°C) and set it up for indirect heat.
2. In a small bowl, combine the smoked paprika, garlic powder, onion powder, dried oregano, salt, and black pepper.
3. Brush the chicken breasts with olive oil on both sides.
4. Sprinkle the spice mixture evenly over the chicken breasts, rubbing it in to ensure full coverage.
5. Place the seasoned chicken breasts on the grill grate, ensuring they are not touching each other.
6. Close the grill lid and smoke the chicken breasts for approximately 1 hour, or until the internal temperature reaches 165°F (74°C).
7. Once cooked, remove the chicken breasts from the grill and let them rest for a few minutes.
8. Slice the smoked chicken breasts and serve them with lemon wedges on the side.

SAVORY-SWEET TURKEY LEGS RECIPE FOR DELICIOUS COMBINATION

Prep Time: 15 minutes | Marinating Time: 4 hours | Cook Time: 2-3 hours | Serves 4

INGREDIENTS

- 4 turkey legs
- 1/4 cup soy sauce
- 2 tablespoons Worcestershire sauce
- 2 tablespoons honey
- 2 tablespoons Dijon mustard
- 2 cloves garlic, minced
- 1 teaspoon dried thyme
- 1 teaspoon smoked paprika
- 1/2 teaspoon salt
- 1/2 teaspoon black pepper

The marinade infuses the turkey legs with rich flavors while keeping them moist and tender. Make sure to marinate the turkey legs for at least 4 hours or overnight for the best results.

INSTRUCTIONS

1. In a bowl, whisk together the soy sauce, Worcestershire sauce, honey, Dijon mustard, minced garlic, dried thyme, smoked paprika, salt, and black pepper to create the marinade.
2. Place the turkey legs in a large resealable bag or container and pour the marinade over them. Ensure that the turkey legs are fully coated. Seal the bag or cover the container and refrigerate for at least 4 hours or overnight for maximum flavor.
3. Preheat your Traeger grill to 325°F (163°C) and set it up for indirect heat.
4. Remove the turkey legs from the marinade, allowing any excess marinade to drip off. Discard the remaining marinade.
5. Place the turkey legs directly on the grill grate, spacing them out for even cooking.
6. Close the grill lid and cook the turkey legs for 2-3 hours, or until the internal temperature reaches 165°F (74°C). Rotate the legs occasionally for even browning.
7. Once cooked, remove the turkey legs from the grill and let them rest for a few minutes before serving.
8. Serve the savory-sweet turkey legs as a main dish alongside your favorite sides such as roasted vegetables, mashed potatoes, or a fresh salad.

DUCK WITH ORANGE-CRANBERRY GLAZE RECIPE

Prep Time: 15 minutes | Marinating Time: 2 hours | Cook Time: 1 hour | Serves 4

INGREDIENTS

- 2 duck breasts
- Salt and pepper to taste
- 1 cup orange juice
- 1/2 cup cranberry sauce
- 2 tablespoons honey
- 1 tablespoon soy sauce
- 1 teaspoon grated orange zest
- 1 teaspoon minced garlic
- 1/2 teaspoon dried thyme
- 1/4 teaspoon ground ginger

The orange-cranberry glaze adds a tangy and sweet touch to the succulent duck breasts. The marinating process helps infuse the flavors and tenderize the meat.

INSTRUCTIONS

1. Pat the duck breasts dry with paper towels and season them with salt and pepper on both sides.
2. Whisk orange juice, cranberry sauce, honey, soy sauce, orange zest, minced garlic, dried thyme, and ground ginger to make the glaze.
3. Marinate duck breasts in half of the glaze in a bag or dish. Reserve the rest for later. Refrigerate for at least 2 hours or overnight for more flavor.
4. Preheat your Traeger grill to 375°F (190°C) and set it up for indirect heat.
5. Remove the duck breasts from the marinade and discard the marinade.
6. Place the duck breasts directly on the grill grate, skin side up. Close the grill lid and cook for 25 minutes.
7. Baste duck after 25 minutes, cook 25-30 more mins until internal temp reaches 135°F (57°C) for medium-rare or 145°F (63°C) for medium. Use meat thermometer.
8. Slice the duck breasts and serve them drizzled with any remaining glaze. Garnish with fresh herbs, if desired.

MINI TURDUCKEN ROULADE FOR UNIQUE POULTRY DELIGHT

Prep Time: 1 hour | Cook Time: 2 hours | Serving Size: 4 servings

INGREDIENTS

- 2 boneless, skinless chicken breasts
- 2 boneless, skinless duck breasts
- 2 boneless, skinless turkey breast cutlets
- Salt and pepper to taste
- 8-10 slices of bacon
- 1/4 cup butter, melted
- 1 tablespoon poultry seasoning
- 1 teaspoon dried thyme
- 1 teaspoon garlic powder
- 1 teaspoon onion powder

he mini turducken roulade offers a combination of flavors from chicken, duck, and turkey, all wrapped in smoky bacon.

INSTRUCTIONS

1. Preheat Traeger grill to 350°F (175°C) for indirect heat.
2. Flatten chicken, duck, and turkey breasts to 1/4-inch thickness.
3. Season flattened breasts with salt and pepper.
4. Stack breasts together, roll tightly into a roulade.
5. Wrap roulade with bacon slices, secure ends.
6. Mix melted butter, poultry seasoning, thyme, garlic powder, and onion powder.
7. Brush butter mixture over roulade.
8. Place roulade on grill, close lid.
9. Cook for about 2 hours until internal temp reaches 165°F (74°C).
10. Let roulade rest for 10 mins.
11. Slice and serve the mini turducken roulade.

WOOD-FIRED CHICKEN BREASTS WITH SMOKY TOUCH

Prep Time: 10 minutes I Cook Time: 25-30 minutes I Serving Size: 4 servings

INGREDIENTS

- 4 boneless, skin-on chicken breasts
- Salt and pepper to taste
- 2 tablespoons olive oil
- 2 teaspoons smoked paprika
- 1 teaspoon garlic powder
- 1 teaspoon onion powder
- 1/2 teaspoon dried oregano
- 1/2 teaspoon dried thyme

 The wood-fired cooking method imparts a smoky flavor to the chicken breasts, enhancing their taste and adding a unique touch to the dish.

INSTRUCTIONS

1. Preheat your Traeger grill to 400°F (200°C) and set it up for direct grilling.
2. Season the chicken breasts generously with salt and pepper on both sides.
3. In a small bowl, mix together the olive oil, smoked paprika, garlic powder, onion powder, dried oregano, and dried thyme to make a marinade.
4. Brush the marinade mixture over the chicken breasts, coating them evenly.
5. Place the chicken breasts directly on the grill grate, skin-side down.
6. Close the grill lid and cook the chicken breasts for 12-15 minutes, or until the skin is crispy and browned.
7. Flip the chicken breasts over and continue cooking for another 10-15 minutes, or until the internal temperature reaches 165°F (74°C) when measured with a meat thermometer inserted into the thickest part of the breasts.
8. Once cooked, remove the chicken breasts from the grill and let them rest for a few minutes before serving.
9. Serve the wood-fired chicken breasts with a smoky touch alongside your favorite side dishes, such as grilled vegetables, roasted potatoes, or a fresh salad.

SMOKED DUCK DRUMSTICKS WITH FLAVORFUL TWIST

Prep Time: 15 minutes I Cook Time: 2.5 to 3 hours I Serving Size: 4 servings

INGREDIENTS

- 4 duck drumsticks
- Salt and pepper to taste
- 2 tablespoons soy sauce
- 2 tablespoons honey
- 2 tablespoons orange juice
- 1 tablespoon Dijon mustard
- 1 teaspoon garlic powder
- 1 teaspoon smoked paprika
- 1/2 teaspoon dried thyme
- 1/2 teaspoon dried rosemary

 Smoking the duck drumsticks infuses them with a rich, smoky flavor that complements the meat's natural richness.

INSTRUCTIONS

1. Preheat your Traeger grill to 225°F (107°C) and set it up for indirect grilling.
2. Season the duck drumsticks with salt and pepper on all sides.
3. Whisk soy sauce, honey, orange juice, Dijon mustard, garlic powder, smoked paprika, dried thyme, and dried rosemary in a small bowl to make marinade.
4. Place the duck drumsticks in a large resealable bag and pour the marinade over them. Seal the bag and massage the marinade into the drumsticks to coat them evenly. Let them marinate in the refrigerator for at least 1 hour, or overnight for maximum flavor.
5. Remove the duck drumsticks from the marinade and discard the excess marinade.
6. Place the drumsticks directly on the grill grate, skin-side up.
7. Smoke drumsticks with closed grill lid for 2.5-3 hours or until internal temp reaches 165°F (74°C) when measured with meat thermometer in thickest part.
8. Once smoked, remove the duck drumsticks from the grill and let them rest for a few minutes before serving.
9. Serve the smoked duck drumsticks with a flavorful twist alongside your favorite side dishes, such as roasted vegetables, wild rice, or a fresh salad.

SMOKED CHICKEN WITH BASIL–FETA SAUCE

Prep Time: 15 minutes | Cook Time: 2 to 2.5 hours | Serving Size: 4 servings

INGREDIENTS

- 4 bone-in chicken breasts
- Salt and pepper to taste
- 2 tablespoons olive oil
- 1/2 cup crumbled feta cheese
- 1/4 cup fresh basil leaves
- 2 cloves garlic, minced
- 2 tablespoons lemon juice
- 1 tablespoon red wine vinegar

Smoking the chicken breasts adds a delicious smoky flavor and keeps the meat tender and juicy. The basil-feta sauce adds a burst of freshness and tanginess to complement the smoky chicken.

INSTRUCTIONS

1. Preheat your Traeger grill to 225°F (107°C) and set it up for indirect grilling.
2. Season the chicken breasts with salt and pepper on all sides.
3. Drizzle the olive oil over the chicken breasts and rub it in to coat them evenly.
4. Place the chicken breasts directly on the grill grate, skin-side up.
5. Close the grill lid and smoke the chicken breasts for 2 to 2.5 hours, or until the internal temperature reaches 165°F (74°C) when measured with a meat thermometer inserted into the thickest part of the breasts.
6. While the chicken is smoking, prepare the basil-feta sauce. In a blender or food processor, combine the crumbled feta cheese, fresh basil leaves, minced garlic, lemon juice, and red wine vinegar. Blend until smooth and creamy.
7. Once the chicken is smoked and cooked through, remove it from the grill and let it rest for a few minutes.
8. Serve the smoked chicken breasts with the basil-feta sauce drizzled over the top.
9. Garnish with additional fresh basil leaves, if desired.

SMOKED DUCK DRUMSTICKS WITH FLAVORFUL TWIST

Prep Time: 15 minutes | Cook Time: 2.5 to 3 hours | Serving Size: 4 servings

INGREDIENTS

- 4 duck drumsticks
- Salt and pepper to taste
- 2 tablespoons soy sauce
- 2 tablespoons honey
- 2 tablespoons orange juice
- 1 tablespoon Dijon mustard
- 1 teaspoon garlic powder
- 1 teaspoon smoked paprika
- 1/2 teaspoon dried thyme
- 1/2 teaspoon dried rosemary

Smoking the duck drumsticks infuses them with a rich, smoky flavor that complements the meat's natural richness.

INSTRUCTIONS

1. Preheat your Traeger grill to 225°F (107°C) and set it up for indirect grilling.
2. Season the duck drumsticks with salt and pepper on all sides.
3. Whisk soy sauce, honey, orange juice, Dijon mustard, garlic powder, smoked paprika, dried thyme, and dried rosemary in a small bowl to make marinade.
4. Place the duck drumsticks in a large resealable bag and pour the marinade over them. Seal the bag and massage the marinade into the drumsticks to coat them evenly. Let them marinate in the refrigerator for at least 1 hour, or overnight for maximum flavor.
5. Remove the duck drumsticks from the marinade and discard the excess marinade.
6. Place the drumsticks directly on the grill grate, skin-side up.
7. Smoke drumsticks with closed grill lid for 2.5-3 hours or until internal temp reaches 165°F (74°C) when measured with meat thermometer in thickest part.
8. Once smoked, remove the duck drumsticks from the grill and let them rest for a few minutes before serving.
9. Serve the smoked duck drumsticks with a flavorful twist alongside your favorite side dishes, such as roasted vegetables, wild rice, or a fresh salad.

CHAPTER 4

FISH AND SEAFOOD

WOOD-FIRED HALIBUT WITH SMOKY FLAVORS

Prep Time: 10 minutes | Cook Time: 12-15 minutes | Serving Size: 4 servings

INGREDIENTS

- 4 halibut fillets (6-8 ounces each)
- Salt and pepper to taste
- 2 tablespoons olive oil
- 1 teaspoon smoked paprika
- 1/2 teaspoon garlic powder
- 1/2 teaspoon onion powder
- 1/2 teaspoon dried thyme
- Lemon wedges, for serving
- Fresh parsley, for garnish

QUICK TIPS
Cooking halibut on a wood-fired grill infuses it with a delightful smoky flavor. The spice rub enhances the natural flavors of the fish and adds a touch of warmth and depth.

INSTRUCTIONS

1. Preheat your Traeger grill to 400°F (204°C) and set it up for direct grilling.
2. Season the halibut fillets with salt and pepper on both sides.
3. In a small bowl, combine the olive oil, smoked paprika, garlic powder, onion powder, and dried thyme. Mix well to create a spice rub.
4. Brush the halibut fillets with the spice rub, coating them evenly on all sides.
5. Place the halibut fillets directly on the grill grate, skin-side down.
6. Close the grill lid and cook the halibut for 12-15 minutes, or until the flesh is opaque and flakes easily with a fork. The internal temperature should reach 145°F (63°C).
7. Carefully remove the halibut from the grill using a spatula and transfer to a serving platter.
8. Squeeze fresh lemon juice over the halibut fillets and garnish with fresh parsley.
9. Serve the wood-fired halibut hot with your favorite side dishes and enjoy the smoky flavors.

PACIFIC NORTHWEST SALMON WITH REGIONAL INFLUENCE

Prep Time: 15 minutes | Marinating Time: 1 hour | Cook Time: 12-15 mins | Serves 4

INGREDIENTS

- 4 salmon fillets (6-8 ounces each)
- 1/4 cup soy sauce
- 1/4 cup maple syrup
- 2 tablespoons Dijon mustard
- 2 tablespoons olive oil
- 2 cloves garlic, minced
- 1 tablespoon fresh lemon juice
- 1 teaspoon smoked paprika
- Salt and pepper to taste
- Lemon wedges, for serving
- Fresh dill, for garnish

QUICK TIPS
This recipe pays homage to the flavors of the Pacific Northwest, combining the richness of salmon with regional ingredients such as maple syrup and Dijon mustard.

INSTRUCTIONS

1. In a bowl, whisk together the soy sauce, maple syrup, Dijon mustard, olive oil, minced garlic, fresh lemon juice, smoked paprika, salt, and pepper.
2. Place the salmon fillets in a shallow dish and pour the marinade over them, ensuring they are well coated. Cover the dish and let the salmon marinate in the refrigerator for at least 1 hour.
3. Preheat your Traeger grill to 400°F (204°C) and set it up for direct grilling.
4. Remove the salmon fillets from the marinade and shake off any excess. Reserve the marinade for basting.
5. Place the salmon fillets directly on the grill grate, skin-side down.
6. Close the grill lid and cook the salmon for 12-15 minutes, or until the flesh is opaque and flakes easily with a fork. Baste the salmon with the reserved marinade occasionally during cooking.
7. Carefully remove the salmon from the grill using a spatula and transfer to a serving platter.
8. Garnish the salmon with fresh dill and serve with lemon wedges on the side.
9. Enjoy the Pacific Northwest salmon with its regional influence, featuring a combination of savory, sweet, and tangy flavors.

CAJUN-BLACKENED SHRIMP WITH SPICY CAJUN SEASONING

Prep Time: 10 minutes | Cook Time: 6 minutes | Serving Size: 4 servings

INGREDIENTS

- 1 pound large shrimp, peeled and deveined
- 2 tablespoons Cajun seasoning
- 1 teaspoon paprika
- 1/2 teaspoon garlic powder
- 1/2 teaspoon onion powder
- 1/2 teaspoon dried thyme
- 1/2 teaspoon dried oregano
- 1/2 teaspoon salt
- 1/4 teaspoon cayenne pepper
- 2 tablespoons olive oil

Cajun seasoning adds a zesty and fiery flavor to the shrimp, while the high heat of the Traeger grill helps achieve the signature blackened crust.

INSTRUCTIONS

1. Mix Cajun seasoning, paprika, garlic powder, onion powder, dried thyme, dried oregano, salt, and cayenne pepper for spicy Cajun seasoning blend.
2. Coat shrimp evenly by drizzling with olive oil and tossing in a large bowl.
3. Coat shrimp with spicy Cajun seasoning, ensuring each shrimp is well covered. Gently rub the seasoning into the shrimp for enhanced flavor.
4. Preheat your Traeger grill to high heat, around 400°F (204°C), and set it up for direct grilling.
5. Place the seasoned shrimp directly on the grill grate in a single layer. Close the grill lid and cook for about 2-3 minutes per side, or until the shrimp turn pink and opaque.
6. Remove the shrimp from the grill and transfer them to a serving platter. Squeeze fresh lemon juice over the shrimp for an extra tangy kick.
7. Garnish the Cajun-blackened shrimp with fresh parsley and serve immediately.
8. Enjoy the succulent and spicy Cajun-blackened shrimp as a flavorful appetizer or main dish.

GRILLED SALMON WITH CHARRED PERFECTION

Prep Time: 10 minutes | Cook Time: 12-15 minutes | Serving Size: 4 servings

INGREDIENTS

- 4 salmon fillets, skin-on
- 2 tablespoons olive oil
- Salt and pepper to taste
- Lemon wedges, for serving
- Fresh dill or parsley, for garnish

Grilling salmon on the Traeger grill adds a smoky and charred flavor to the fish, elevating its taste. Make sure to oil the grill grates before cooking to prevent sticking.

INSTRUCTIONS

1. Preheat your Traeger grill to medium-high heat, around 400°F (204°C), and set it up for direct grilling.
2. Brush the salmon fillets with olive oil on both sides. This will help prevent sticking and add flavor.
3. Season the salmon fillets with salt and pepper, ensuring that both sides are evenly coated.
4. Place the salmon fillets, skin-side down, directly on the grill grate. Close the grill lid and cook for 6-8 minutes, or until the skin is crispy and charred.
5. Carefully flip the salmon fillets using a spatula. Close the grill lid and continue cooking for another 4-6 minutes, or until the salmon is cooked through and flakes easily with a fork.
6. Remove the grilled salmon from the grill and transfer them to a serving platter. Squeeze fresh lemon juice over the salmon to enhance the flavors.
7. Garnish the grilled salmon with fresh dill or parsley for a pop of freshness.
8. Serve the charred salmon immediately with additional lemon wedges on the side.
9. Enjoy the perfectly grilled salmon with its crispy skin and tender, flaky flesh.

BBQ SMOKED SALMON WITH SMOKY BARBECUE TWIST

Prep Time: 10 minutes | Marinating Time: 1 hour | Cook Time: 1 hour | Serving Size: 4

INGREDIENTS

- 1 pound salmon fillet, skin-on
- 2 tablespoons brown sugar
- 2 tablespoons paprika
- 1 tablespoon chili powder
- 1 teaspoon garlic powder
- 1 teaspoon onion powder
- 1 teaspoon salt
- 1/2 teaspoon black pepper
- 2 tablespoons olive oil
- 1/4 cup barbecue sauce

INSTRUCTIONS

1. Preheat Traeger grill to 225°F (107°C) for indirect heat smoking.
2. Combine brown sugar, paprika, chili powder, garlic powder, onion powder, salt, black pepper, and cayenne pepper (optional) for the dry rub.
3. Place salmon on aluminum foil, drizzle with olive oil, and coat evenly.
4. Sprinkle dry rub mixture over salmon, pressing gently to adhere.
5. Let salmon marinate with the dry rub for 1 hour.
6. Place foil with salmon on grill grate, skin-side down.
7. Smoke salmon for about 1 hour until internal temp reaches 145°F (63°C).
8. Brush barbecue sauce over salmon in the last 10 minutes of cooking.
9. Remove salmon from grill and transfer to serving platter.
10. Let salmon rest before slicing and serving.

QUICK TIPS Smoking salmon on a Traeger grill imparts a rich and smoky flavor. Make sure to monitor the internal temperature of the salmon to prevent overcooking.

HOT SMOKED SALMON WITH INTENSE SMOKY AROMAS

Prep Time: 15 minutes | Brining Time: 2 hours | Cook Time: 1-2 hours | Serving Size: 4

INGREDIENTS

- 1 pound salmon fillet, skin-on
- 1/4 cup kosher salt
- 1/4 cup brown sugar
- 1 tablespoon black peppercorns
- 1 tablespoon coriander seeds
- 1 tablespoon mustard seeds
- 1 tablespoon smoked paprika
- 1 teaspoon garlic powder
- 1 teaspoon onion powder

INSTRUCTIONS

1. Combine kosher salt, brown sugar, black peppercorns, coriander seeds, mustard seeds, smoked paprika, garlic powder, and onion powder in a mixing bowl for the dry brine mixture.
2. Place salmon in dish or on baking sheet, pat dry with paper towel.
3. Sprinkle dry brine mixture over salmon, covering all sides. Press gently into flesh.
4. Cover with plastic wrap, refrigerate for at least 2 hours.
5. Preheat Traeger grill to 225°F (107°C) for hot smoking.
6. Soak wood chips/chunks in water for 30 mins, drain well.
7. Add drained wood chips/chunks to smoker box or foil packet on grill.
8. Place salmon on grill grate, skin-side down.
9. Close lid, smoke salmon for 1-2 hours until internal temp is 145°F (63°C) and flesh is opaque and flaky.
10. Carefully remove smoked salmon from grill, transfer to serving platter.
11. Let salmon cool briefly before serving.
12. Serve as main dish or use in salads, sandwiches, or pasta dishes.

QUICK TIPS Hot smoking salmon on a Traeger grill creates intense smoky aromas and flavors. The dry brine helps to season the salmon and enhance its natural taste.

SEARED TUNA STEAKS WITH SEAR MARKS AND FLAVORFUL CENTER

Prep Time: 15 minutes I Cook Time: 6-8 minutes I Serving Size: 2

INGREDIENTS

- 2 tuna steaks, about 6 ounces each
- 2 tablespoons soy sauce
- 1 tablespoon olive oil
- 1 tablespoon sesame oil
- 1 tablespoon lemon juice
- 1 teaspoon minced garlic
- 1 teaspoon grated ginger
- Salt and pepper, to taste
- Sesame seeds, for garnish

 Tuna steaks cook quickly, so it's important to monitor their internal temperature for the desired level of doneness.

INSTRUCTIONS

1. Mix soy sauce, olive oil, sesame oil, lemon juice, minced garlic, grated ginger, salt, and pepper in shallow dish.
2. Coat tuna steaks in marinade, let marinate for 10 mins at room temp or up to 30 mins in fridge.
3. Preheat Traeger grill to high heat (450°F/232°C).
4. Remove tuna from marinade, allowing excess to drip off.
5. Place tuna steaks on grill grates.
6. Sear for 2-3 mins per side, rotating 90 degrees halfway for grill marks.
7. Avoid moving or pressing down on tuna while searing.
8. Use meat thermometer, aim for internal temp of 125-130°F (52-54°C) for medium-rare.
9. Remove tuna from grill, let rest on cutting board.
10. Allow tuna to rest briefly before slicing.
11. Slice tuna against the grain into thin slices.
12. Sprinkle with sesame seeds and garnish with green onions if desired.
13. Serve immediately as main dish or with salad or rice.

BARBECUED SHRIMP WITH GRILLED GOODNESS

Prep Time: 15 minutes I Marinating Time: 30 mins I Cook Time: 5-7 minutes I Serving Size: 4

INGREDIENTS

- 1 pound large shrimp, peeled and deveined
- 2 tablespoons olive oil
- 2 tablespoons lemon juice
- 2 cloves garlic, minced
- 1 teaspoon paprika
- 1/2 teaspoon cayenne pepper
- 1/2 teaspoon black pepper
- 1/2 teaspoon salt
- 1/4 cup barbecue sauce
- Fresh parsley, chopped (for garnish)

 Be cautious not to overcook the shrimp, as they can become rubbery. Adjust the grilling time based on the size of your shrimp.

INSTRUCTIONS

1. Combine olive oil, lemon juice, minced garlic, paprika, cayenne pepper, black pepper, and salt in a bowl for marinade.
2. Coat shrimp in marinade, refrigerate for 30 mins.
3. Preheat Traeger grill to medium-high heat (400°F/204°C).
4. Remove shrimp from marinade, keep marinade aside.
5. Thread shrimp onto skewers, leaving space between each.
6. Place skewered shrimp on grill grates.
7. Cook shrimp for 2-3 mins on each side until pink and opaque.
8. Brush shrimp with reserved marinade and turn occasionally for even cooking and flavor.
9. Once cooked and grilled, remove shrimp from grill.
10. Brush barbecued shrimp with barbecue sauce, coating evenly.
11. Transfer shrimp to serving platter, garnish with parsley.
12. Serve immediately as appetizer or part of main course with rice, grilled vegetables, or salad.
13. Enjoy the succulent barbecued shrimp with their grilled goodness.

LOBSTER TAILS WITH HERB BUTTER FOR LUXURIOUS DELIGHT

Prep Time: 15 minutes | Cook Time: 10-12 minutes | Serving Size: 2

INGREDIENTS

- 2 lobster tails

- 4 tablespoons unsalted butter, softened

- 2 cloves garlic, minced

- 2 tablespoons fresh parsley, finely chopped

- 1 tablespoon fresh lemon juice

- 1/2 teaspoon salt

- 1/4 teaspoon black pepper

- Lemon wedges, for serving

Adjust the cooking time based on the size of your lobster tails. The herb butter adds richness and enhances the natural flavors of the lobster meat.

INSTRUCTIONS

1. Preheat Traeger grill to medium-high heat (400°F/204°C).
2. Carefully cut top shell of lobster tails, starting from open end towards the tail.
3. Pry open shell, rest lobster meat on top, leaving tail intact.
4. Mix softened butter, minced garlic, chopped parsley, lemon juice, salt, and black pepper in a bowl to make herb butter.
5. Spoon herb butter over lobster meat, ensuring even coverage.
6. Place lobster tails on grill grates, meat side up.
7. Close lid, cook for 10-12 mins until meat is opaque and firm.
8. Occasionally baste lobster tails with drippings or melted herb butter.
9. Carefully remove lobster tails from grill with tongs.
10. Serve immediately with lemon wedges.
11. Use fork to separate meat from shell, dip in herb butter for extra flavor.
12. Enjoy the deliciousness of grilled lobster tails with herb butter.

OYSTERS IN THE SHELL WITH FRESH SEA FLAVORS

Prep Time: 10 minutes | Cook Time: 10 minutes | Serving Size: 4

INGREDIENTS

- 12 fresh oysters, in the shell

- 4 tablespoons unsalted butter, melted

- 2 cloves garlic, minced

- 2 tablespoons fresh parsley, finely chopped

- 1 tablespoon fresh lemon juice

- Salt and pepper, to taste

- Lemon wedges, for serving

It's crucial to use fresh, live oysters for this recipe. Discard any oysters that are already open or don't close when tapped.

INSTRUCTIONS

1. Preheat Traeger grill to high heat (450°F/232°C).
2. Clean oyster shells under cold water to remove debris.
3. Carefully open oyster shells using oyster knife or paring knife.
4. Mix melted butter, minced garlic, chopped parsley, lemon juice, salt, and pepper in a bowl to make flavored butter.
5. Place opened oyster shells on grill grates.
6. Spoon flavored butter onto each oyster, distributing evenly.
7. Close lid, cook oysters for 8-10 mins until edges curl and oysters are cooked.
8. Watch closely to prevent overcooking.
9. Carefully remove grilled oysters from grill with tongs or heatproof glove.
10. Serve immediately on platter, garnished with parsley and lemon wedges.
11. Use oyster fork or small fork to loosen oyster from shell, then slurp directly from shell.
12. Squeeze fresh lemon juice over oyster before eating.
13. Enjoy the deliciousness of grilled oysters with their fresh sea flavors.

GRILLED KING CRAB LEGS WITH BUTTERY GOODNESS

Prep Time: 10 minutes | Cook Time: 10-15 minutes | Serving Size: 4

INGREDIENTS

- 2 pounds king crab legs, thawed if frozen
- 1/2 cup unsalted butter, melted
- 2 cloves garlic, minced
- 2 tablespoons fresh lemon juice
- 1 tablespoon fresh parsley, chopped
- Salt and pepper, to taste
- Lemon wedges, for serving

 Make sure the king crab legs are fully thawed before grilling if they were frozen. The buttery sauce adds richness and enhances the natural flavors of the crab meat.

INSTRUCTIONS

1. Preheat Traeger grill to medium-high heat (400°F/204°C).
2. Carefully cut along shell of each crab leg to expose meat.
3. Mix melted butter, minced garlic, lemon juice, chopped parsley, salt, and pepper in a bowl for buttery sauce.
4. Brush crab legs generously with buttery sauce, coating evenly.
5. Place crab legs on grill grates.
6. Close lid, cook for 10-15 mins until meat is heated through and opaque.
7. Occasionally baste crab legs with more buttery sauce while grilling.
8. Carefully remove grilled crab legs from grill with tongs or heatproof glove.
9. Transfer grilled crab legs to serving platter, drizzle with remaining buttery sauce.
10. Serve hot with lemon wedges for squeezing over meat.
11. Use crab cracker or seafood fork to crack open shells and extract crab meat.
12. Dip crab meat in buttery sauce or enjoy as is.
13. Enjoy the succulent flavors of grilled king crab legs with their buttery goodness.

CHARLESTON CRAB CAKES WITH REMOULADE FOR SOUTHERN DELIGHT

Prep Time: 20 minutes | Cook Time: 10 minutes | Serving Size: 4

INGREDIENTS

- 1 pound lump crab meat
- 1/2 cup bread crumbs
- 1/4 cup mayonnaise
- 2 tablespoons Dijon mustard
- 1 tablespoon Worcestershire sauce
- 1 tablespoon Old Bay seasoning
- 1/4 cup finely chopped green onions
- 1/4 cup finely chopped red bell pepper
- 2 tablespoons chopped fresh parsley
- Salt and pepper, to taste
- Vegetable oil, for frying

 Refrigerating the crab cakes before grilling helps them hold their shape. Adjust the cooking time based on the thickness of the crab cakes.

INSTRUCTIONS

1. Combine lump crab meat, bread crumbs, mayonnaise, Dijon mustard, Worcestershire sauce, Old Bay seasoning, green onions, red bell pepper, parsley, salt, and pepper in a bowl.
2. Shape mixture into 8 crab cakes, about 3 inches in diameter and 1/2 inch thick.
3. Refrigerate crab cakes on parchment-lined baking sheet for 30 mins.
4. Preheat Traeger grill to medium-high heat (375°F/190°C).
5. Brush grill grates with vegetable oil.
6. Place crab cakes on grill grates, cook 4-5 mins per side until golden brown and heated through.
7. Whisk mayonnaise, Dijon mustard, parsley, capers, dill pickle, shallot, Worcestershire sauce, hot sauce, salt, and pepper for remoulade sauce.
8. Transfer grilled crab cakes to serving platter.
9. Serve hot with remoulade sauce for dipping or drizzling.
10. Enjoy flavorful and crispy Charleston crab cakes with tangy remoulade sauce.

CITRUS-SMOKED TROUT WITH TANGY CITRUS NOTES

Prep Time: 10 minutes | Marinating Time: 30 minutes | Cook Time: 20 minutes | Serving Size: 4

INGREDIENTS

- 4 trout fillets
- 2 tablespoons olive oil
- 2 tablespoons lemon juice
- 2 tablespoons orange juice
- 1 tablespoon lime juice
- Zest of 1 lemon
- Zest of 1 orange
- Zest of 1 lime
- 1 teaspoon paprika
- 1 teaspoon garlic powder
- 1 teaspoon dried thyme

 Make sure to remove any pin bones from the trout fillets before marinating.

INSTRUCTIONS

1. Whisk olive oil, lemon juice, orange juice, lime juice, lemon zest, orange zest, lime zest, paprika, garlic powder, dried thyme, salt, and pepper in a bowl.
2. Place trout fillets in shallow dish, pour citrus marinade over them, ensuring even coating. Marinate in fridge for at least 30 mins.
3. Preheat Traeger grill to medium heat (350°F/175°C).
4. Remove trout fillets from marinade, discard excess liquid.
5. Place trout fillets on grill grates, skin-side down.
6. Close lid, smoke trout for about 20 mins until flesh is opaque and flakes easily with a fork. Adjust cooking time based on fillet thickness.
7. Carefully remove trout from grill, transfer to serving platter.
8. Garnish trout with additional citrus slices for vibrant presentation.
9. Serve hot, allowing tangy citrus notes to enhance fish flavor.
10. Enjoy succulent and smoky citrus-smoked trout with refreshing citrus flavors.

BARBECUED SCALLOPS WITH GRILLED PERFECTION

Prep Time: 15 minutes | Marinating Time: 30 minutes | Cook Time: 5-7 mins | Serving Size: 4

INGREDIENTS

- 1 pound fresh scallops
- 2 tablespoons olive oil
- 2 tablespoons lemon juice
- 2 cloves garlic, minced
- 1 teaspoon smoked paprika
- 1 teaspoon dried thyme
- Salt and pepper, to taste
- Skewers (if using wooden skewers, soak them in water for 30 minutes before grilling)
- Lemon wedges, for serving
- Fresh parsley, chopped, for garnish

 Ensure that the scallops are dry before marinating to help them sear properly. Be careful not to overcrowd the skewers to ensure even cooking.

INSTRUCTIONS

1. Whisk olive oil, lemon juice, minced garlic, smoked paprika, dried thyme, salt, and pepper in a bowl for marinade.
2. Place scallops in shallow dish, pour marinade over them, ensuring even coating. Marinate in fridge for at least 30 mins.
3. Preheat Traeger grill to medium-high heat (400°F/200°C).
4. Thread scallops onto skewers, leaving gap between each for even cooking.
5. Place skewered scallops on grill grates.
6. Close lid, cook scallops for 2-3 mins per side until opaque with grill marks. Avoid overcooking for tenderness.
7. Remove scallops from grill, transfer to serving platter.
8. Squeeze fresh lemon juice over scallops, sprinkle with chopped parsley.
9. Serve hot as appetizer or main dish.
10. Enjoy succulent and perfectly grilled scallops with side of salad or grilled vegetables.

CURED COLD-SMOKED LOX WITH CLASSIC PREPARATION

Prep Time: 20 minutes | Curing Time: 24 hours | Smoking Time: 6-8 hours | Serving Size: 4

INGREDIENTS

- 1 pound fresh salmon fillet, skin-on

- 1/4 cup kosher salt

- 1/4 cup granulated sugar

- 1 tablespoon black peppercorns, crushed

- 1 tablespoon coriander seeds, crushed

- 1 tablespoon dill seeds

- Zest of 1 lemon

- Zest of 1 orange

- Wood chips for smoking (e.g., alder, hickory, or apple)

 Cold smoking requires a low temperature to infuse the salmon with smoky flavors without cooking it.

INSTRUCTIONS

1. Rinse salmon fillet, pat dry. Place on cutting board.
2. Mix kosher salt, granulated sugar, crushed black peppercorns, crushed coriander seeds, dill seeds, lemon zest, and orange zest for curing mixture.
3. Sprinkle curing mixture generously over all sides of salmon, coating evenly.
4. Place salmon in glass dish or on rimmed baking sheet. Cover tightly with plastic wrap, refrigerate for 24 hours.
5. After 24 hours, rinse off curing mixture under cold water. Pat dry.
6. Preheat Traeger grill to 180°F (82°C) for cold smoking.
7. Soak wood chips in water for 30 mins.
8. Drain wood chips, place in smoker box or foil packet with holes.
9. Place cured salmon directly on grill grate, skin-side down.
10. Close lid, cold smoke salmon for 6-8 hours, replenishing wood chips as needed.
11. Once cold smoking is complete, remove salmon from grill, let cool to room temp.
12. Slice cold-smoked salmon thinly at an angle for serving.
13. Serve with bagels, cream cheese, sliced red onions, capers, and fresh dill.

DIJON-SMOKED HALIBUT WITH MUSTARD INFUSION

Prep Time: 15 minutes | Marinating Time: 1 hour | Cook Time: 15 minutes | Serving Size: 4

INGREDIENTS

- 4 halibut fillets, about 6 ounces each

- 2 tablespoons Dijon mustard

- 2 tablespoons olive oil

- 2 tablespoons lemon juice

- 1 tablespoon honey

- 1 teaspoon smoked paprika

- 1 teaspoon garlic powder

- 1 teaspoon salt

- 1/2 teaspoon black pepper

 Adjust the cooking time based on the thickness of the halibut fillets. The halibut is cooked when it turns opaque and easily flakes with a fork.

INSTRUCTIONS

1. Whisk Dijon mustard, olive oil, lemon juice, honey, smoked paprika, garlic powder, salt, and black pepper for marinade.
2. Place halibut fillets in shallow dish or resealable plastic bag. Pour marinade over fillets, ensuring even coating. Refrigerate for 1 hour.
3. Soak wood chips in water for at least 30 mins.
4. Preheat Traeger grill to 350°F (175°C) for medium-high heat smoking.
5. Drain wood chips, place in smoker box or foil packet with holes.
6. Remove halibut fillets from marinade, let excess drip off. Discard remaining marinade.
7. Place halibut fillets on grill grate, skin-side down.
8. Close lid, smoke halibut for about 15 mins until internal temp reaches 145°F (63°C) and flakes easily with a fork.
9. Carefully remove halibut from grill, transfer to serving platter.
10. Let halibut rest briefly before serving.
11. Serve with favorite side dishes like roasted vegetables, rice, or salad.
12. Enjoy tender and flavorful Dijon-smoked halibut with delicious mustard infusion.

SUMMER PAELLA WITH SEASONAL SEAFOOD AND SAFFRON

Prep Time: 20 minutes I Cook Time: 45 minutes I Serving Size: 4-6

INGREDIENTS

- 2 tablespoons olive oil
- 1 onion, diced
- 2 cloves garlic, minced
- 1 red bell pepper, diced
- 1 yellow bell pepper, diced
- 1 cup Arborio rice
- 1 teaspoon smoked paprika
- 1/2 teaspoon saffron threads
- 1/2 teaspoon turmeric
- 4 cups chicken or vegetable broth
- 1 cup white wine
- 1 pound mixed seafood
- 1 cup frozen peas
- 1 lemon, cut into wedges

INSTRUCTIONS

1. Preheat Traeger grill to medium-high heat.
2. Heat olive oil in large paella pan or skillet. Sauté diced onion and minced garlic until softened and fragrant.
3. Add diced red and yellow bell peppers, cook for 2-3 mins until softened.
4. Stir in Arborio rice, smoked paprika, saffron threads, and turmeric. Toast for 1-2 mins to coat rice.
5. Pour in chicken or vegetable broth and white wine, bring to simmer.
6. Transfer paella pan to preheated grill, close lid, cook for 25-30 mins until rice is tender and most liquid is absorbed. Stir occasionally.
7. Clean and devein shrimp, scrub mussels and clams.
8. After 25-30 mins, open grill lid, add seafood and frozen peas to paella pan. Push seafood into rice mixture. Close lid, cook for 10-15 mins until seafood is cooked and shells open.
9. Remove paella pan from grill. Squeeze lemon juice, garnish with parsley.
10. Season with salt and pepper, give paella a gentle stir.
11. Serve directly from pan, garnish with lemon wedges.

LEMON PEPPER WHOLE TROUT WITH BRIGHT CITRUS SEASONING

Prep Time: 10 minutes I Cook Time: 15-20 minutes I Serving Size: 2-4

INGREDIENTS

- 2 whole trout, cleaned and gutted
- 2 lemons, sliced
- 2 tablespoons olive oil
- 1 teaspoon lemon zest
- 1 teaspoon black pepper
- 1 teaspoon salt
- Fresh parsley, chopped, for garnish

INSTRUCTIONS

1. Preheat your Traeger grill to medium-high heat.
2. Rinse the trout under cold water and pat dry with paper towels.
3. Drizzle olive oil over both sides of the trout, ensuring they are evenly coated.
4. In a small bowl, combine the lemon zest, black pepper, and salt. Mix well to create the lemon pepper seasoning.
5. Sprinkle the lemon pepper seasoning over both sides of the trout, rubbing it gently to adhere to the skin.
6. Stuff the cavity of each trout with lemon slices, placing a few slices inside.
7. Place the trout directly on the grill grate, skin-side down.
8. Close the grill lid and cook the trout for 15-20 minutes, or until the flesh is opaque and easily flakes with a fork. The exact cooking time may vary depending on the size of the trout.
9. Once the trout is cooked, carefully remove them from the grill using a spatula.
10. Transfer the trout to a serving platter and garnish with fresh chopped parsley.
11. Serve the lemon pepper whole trout immediately, squeezing additional lemon juice over the top if desired.
12. Enjoy the bright and citrusy flavors of the lemon pepper whole trout.

QUICK TIPS

Make sure to clean and gut the trout thoroughly before cooking. Adjust the cooking time based on the size and thickness of the trout.

CAJUN CATFISH WITH SPICY SOUTHERN FLAVORS

Prep Time: 10 minutes | Cook Time: 10-12 minutes | Serving Size: 4

INGREDIENTS

- 4 catfish fillets
- 2 tablespoons Cajun seasoning
- 1 tablespoon paprika
- 1 teaspoon garlic powder
- 1 teaspoon onion powder
- 1/2 teaspoon cayenne pepper
- 1/2 teaspoon black pepper
- 1/2 teaspoon salt
- 2 tablespoons olive oil
- Lemon wedges, for serving
- Fresh parsley, chopped, for garnish

 Adjust the amount of cayenne pepper according to your spice preference. Feel free to add additional Cajun seasoning or spices to enhance the flavor.

INSTRUCTIONS

1. Preheat your Traeger grill to medium-high heat.
2. In a small bowl, combine the Cajun seasoning, paprika, garlic powder, onion powder, cayenne pepper, black pepper, and salt. Mix well to create the spice rub.
3. Pat dry the catfish fillets with paper towels to remove any excess moisture.
4. Drizzle the olive oil over both sides of the catfish fillets, ensuring they are evenly coated.
5. Sprinkle the spice rub over both sides of the catfish fillets, pressing it gently to adhere to the surface.
6. Place the catfish fillets directly on the grill grate.
7. Close the grill lid and cook the catfish for 5-6 minutes per side, or until the fish is opaque and easily flakes with a fork. The cooking time may vary depending on the thickness of the fillets.
8. Once cooked, carefully remove the catfish fillets from the grill using a spatula.
9. Transfer the catfish to a serving platter and garnish with fresh chopped parsley.
10. Serve the Cajun catfish hot with lemon wedges on the side for squeezing over the fish.

GARLIC-SOY TUNA STEAKS WITH ASIAN-INSPIRED TWIST

Prep Time: 15 mins | Marinating Time: 30 mins | Cook Time: 6-8 mins | Serving Size: 4

INGREDIENTS

- 4 tuna steaks (6-8 ounces each)
- 1/4 cup soy sauce
- 2 tablespoons sesame oil
- 2 tablespoons rice vinegar
- 2 tablespoons honey
- 3 cloves garlic, minced
- 1 teaspoon grated fresh ginger
- 1/2 teaspoon red pepper flakes (optional)
- 2 green onions, sliced (for garnish)
- Sesame seeds (for garnish)

 Be careful not to marinate the tuna for too long, as the acidity in the marinade can start to break down the fish.

INSTRUCTIONS

1. Whisk soy sauce, sesame oil, rice vinegar, honey, minced garlic, grated ginger, and red pepper flakes for marinade.
2. Place tuna steaks in shallow dish or resealable plastic bag. Pour marinade over steaks, fully coating. Refrigerate for at least 30 mins.
3. Preheat Traeger grill to high heat.
4. Remove tuna steaks from marinade, allowing excess to drip off.
5. Place tuna steaks directly on grill grates.
6. Grill for 3-4 mins per side for medium-rare, adjusting cooking time for desired doneness. Avoid overcooking for tenderness.
7. Optionally, brush tuna with leftover marinade while grilling for enhanced flavor.
8. Remove tuna steaks from grill, transfer to serving platter.
9. Garnish with sliced green onions and sprinkle with sesame seeds.
10. Serve hot as main dish, pairing with steamed rice and stir-fried vegetables.
11. Enjoy tender and flavorful garlic-soy tuna steaks with Asian-inspired twist.

SPICY BBQ SHRIMP WITH FIERY BARBECUE SAUCE

Prep Time: 15 mins | Marinating Time: 30 mins | Cook Time: 6-8 mins | Serving Size: 4

INGREDIENTS

- 1 pound large shrimp, peeled and deveined
- 2 tablespoons olive oil
- 2 tablespoons lemon juice
- 2 cloves garlic, minced
- 1 teaspoon paprika
- 1/2 teaspoon cayenne pepper
- 1/2 teaspoon smoked paprika
- 1/2 teaspoon black pepper
- 1/4 teaspoon salt
- 1/4 cup barbecue sauce (your preferred spicy variety)
- 2 tablespoons honey
- Fresh parsley, chopped (for garnish)
- Lemon wedges (for serving)

INSTRUCTIONS

1. Combine olive oil, lemon juice, minced garlic, paprika, cayenne pepper, smoked paprika, black pepper, and salt for marinade.
2. Toss shrimp in marinade, refrigerate for 30 mins.
3. Preheat Traeger grill to medium-high heat.
4. Mix barbecue sauce and honey in small saucepan, heat until warmed.
5. Thread marinated shrimp onto skewers.
6. Place shrimp skewers on grill grates.
7. Grill shrimp for 2-3 mins per side until pink and opaque.
8. Brush shrimp with spicy barbecue sauce while grilling.
9. Continue grilling, basting with sauce, for 1-2 mins until nicely glazed and slightly charred.
10. Remove shrimp skewers from grill, transfer to serving platter.
11. Garnish with fresh chopped parsley.
12. Serve hot as appetizer or main dish, with lemon wedges for squeezing.
13. Enjoy fiery and flavorful BBQ shrimp with a spicy kick.

BLACKENED FISH TACOS WITH BOLD AND SPICY FLAVORS

Prep Time: 15 minutes | Cook Time: 10 minutes | Serving Size: 4

INGREDIENTS

- 1 tablespoon paprika
- 1 tablespoon garlic powder
- 1 tablespoon onion powder
- 1 tablespoon dried thyme
- 1 tablespoon dried oregano
- 1 teaspoon cayenne pepper
- 1 teaspoon black pepper
- 1 teaspoon salt

INSTRUCTIONS

1. Mix ingredients for blackening spice in a small bowl. Set aside.
2. Pat fish fillets dry, rub with blackening spice on both sides.
3. Preheat Traeger grill to medium-high heat.
4. Brush grill grates with vegetable oil.
5. Place seasoned fish fillets on grill, cook for 4-5 mins per side until cooked through and flaky.
6. Prepare spicy mayo by combining mayonnaise, hot sauce, and lime juice. Adjust hot sauce to taste.
7. Warm corn tortillas on grill for 30 secs per side until soft.
8. Remove cooked fish from grill, let it rest, then flake with a fork.
9. Assemble tacos with spicy mayo, shredded lettuce, diced tomatoes, sliced avocado, and grilled blackened fish.
10. Garnish with chopped cilantro, squeeze lime juice.
11. Serve tacos immediately while warm.
12. Enjoy bold and spicy flavors of blackened fish tacos!

QUICK TIPS

You can adjust the level of spiciness by adding more or less cayenne pepper and hot sauce to the blackening spice and spicy mayo.

GINGER-SOY MAHIMAHI WITH BANG BANG SAUCE FOR FUSION DELIGHT

Prep Time: 15 mins | Marinating Time: 30 mins | Cook Time: 10 mins | Serving Size: 4

INGREDIENTS

- 1/4 cup soy sauce
- 2 tablespoons rice vinegar
- 2 tablespoons honey
- 1 tablespoon grated fresh ginger
- 2 cloves garlic, minced
- 1 tablespoon sesame oil
- 1 tablespoon lime juice

You can substitute mahimahi with other firm-fleshed fish like tuna or swordfish. Adjust the grilling time accordingly based on the thickness of the fillets.

INSTRUCTIONS

1. Whisk ginger-soy marinade ingredients together in a small bowl.
2. Marinate mahimahi fillets in the mixture for at least 30 minutes.
3. Make bang bang sauce by combining ingredients, adjusting sweetness and spiciness to taste.
4. Preheat Traeger grill to medium-high heat.
5. Season marinated mahimahi fillets with salt and pepper.
6. Brush grill grates with vegetable oil.
7. Grill mahimahi for 4-5 minutes per side, until opaque and flaky.
8. Warm bang bang sauce in a saucepan or microwave.
9. Transfer grilled mahimahi to a serving platter.
10. Drizzle mahimahi with bang bang sauce.
11. Garnish with cilantro and sesame seeds.
12. Serve ginger-soy mahimahi with bang bang sauce immediately, with lime wedges on the side.
13. Enjoy the delicious fusion of flavors!

BOURBON-CANDIED SALMON BITES WITH SWEET AND SAVORY BLEND

Prep Time: 15 minutes | Marinating Time: 1 hour | Cook Time: 15 minutes | Serving Size: 4

INGREDIENTS

- 1 pound salmon fillet, skin removed
- 1/4 cup bourbon
- 2 tablespoons brown sugar
- 2 tablespoons soy sauce
- 1 tablespoon Dijon mustard
- 1 teaspoon garlic powder
- 1/2 teaspoon smoked paprika
- 1/4 teaspoon cayenne pepper
- Salt and pepper, to taste

You can adjust the amount of bourbon and cayenne pepper according to your preference for sweetness and spiciness.

INSTRUCTIONS

1. Whisk bourbon, brown sugar, soy sauce, Dijon mustard, garlic powder, smoked paprika, cayenne pepper (optional), salt, and pepper in a small bowl.
2. Marinate salmon in the mixture for at least 1 hour.
3. Preheat Traeger grill to medium-high heat.
4. Mix brown sugar, maple syrup, and Dijon mustard for the candied glaze.
5. Remove salmon from marinade, reserving it for basting.
6. Place salmon on grill grates and cook for 5 minutes, then flip.
7. Brush salmon with reserved marinade and continue grilling for another 5 minutes.
8. Brush candied glaze over salmon and cook for 3-5 more minutes until caramelized.
9. Remove salmon from grill and let it rest.
10. Cut salmon into bite-sized pieces and arrange on a serving platter.
11. Garnish with parsley or cilantro (optional) and sesame seeds.
12. Serve as appetizers or part of a main dish.
13. Enjoy the delectable blend of sweet and savory flavors!

CRAB CAKES WITH SPICY MAYO FOR ZESTY SEAFOOD TREAT

Prep Time: 20 minutes | Cook Time: 10 minutes | Serving Size: 4

INGREDIENTS

- 1 pound lump crab meat
- 1/2 cup breadcrumbs
- 1/4 cup mayonnaise
- 2 green onions, finely chopped
- 1/4 cup red bell pepper, finely chopped
- 1/4 cup celery, finely chopped
- 1 tablespoon Dijon mustard
- 1 tablespoon fresh lemon juice
- 1 teaspoon Old Bay seasoning
- Salt and pepper, to taste
- 2 tablespoons vegetable oil, for frying

INSTRUCTIONS

1. Combine crab meat, breadcrumbs, mayonnaise, green onions, red bell pepper, celery, mustard, lemon juice, Old Bay seasoning, salt, and pepper in a bowl.
2. Shape mixture into crab cakes and place on a lined baking sheet.
3. Chill crab cakes in the refrigerator for 30 minutes.
4. Mix mayonnaise, sriracha sauce, lemon juice, garlic powder, salt, and pepper for spicy mayo.
5. Heat oil in a skillet over medium-high heat.
6. Cook crab cakes in the skillet for 4-5 minutes per side until golden and crispy.
7. Drain cooked crab cakes on paper towels.
8. Serve warm with a dollop of spicy mayo.
9. Enjoy the flavorful crab cakes with spicy mayo.

QUICK TIPS Make sure to handle the crab meat gently to keep the lumps intact. Adjust the seasoning and spices according to your taste preferences.

CAJUN AND GARLIC BUTTER SHRIMP PASTA WITH BOLD FLAVORS

Prep Time: 15 minutes | Cook Time: 20 minutes | Serving Size: 4

INGREDIENTS

- 8 ounces linguine or spaghetti
- 1 pound shrimp, peeled and deveined
- 2 tablespoons Cajun seasoning
- 4 tablespoons unsalted butter
- 4 cloves garlic, minced
- 1 cup chicken broth
- 1 cup heavy cream
- 1/2 cup grated Parmesan cheese
- Salt and pepper, to taste
- Fresh parsley, chopped

INSTRUCTIONS

1. Cook pasta until al dente, then set aside.
2. Toss shrimp with Cajun seasoning in a bowl.
3. Melt butter in a skillet over medium-high heat, add minced garlic, and cook until fragrant.
4. Cook seasoned shrimp in the skillet for 2-3 minutes per side until pink and cooked through. Set aside.
5. Add chicken broth to the skillet and simmer for 2-3 minutes.
6. Reduce heat to medium and add heavy cream, stirring to combine.
7. Stir in grated Parmesan cheese until melted and smooth. Season with salt and pepper.
8. Add cooked pasta to the skillet and toss to coat in the sauce.
9. Add shrimp back to the skillet and gently toss to combine.
10. Cook for an additional 1-2 minutes until heated through.
11. Remove from heat and garnish with fresh parsley.
12. Serve immediately. Enjoy the Cajun and garlic butter shrimp pasta.

QUICK TIPS You can also add additional ingredients like diced bell peppers, onions, or cherry tomatoes for added flavor and texture.

LOBSTER TAIL WITH BUTTERY GOODNESS AND DELICATE MEAT

Prep Time: 10 minutes I Cook Time: 15 minutes I Serving Size: 4

INGREDIENTS

- 2 lobster tails

- 4 tablespoons unsalted butter, melted

- 2 cloves garlic, minced

- 1 tablespoon fresh lemon juice

- Salt and pepper, to taste

- Fresh parsley, chopped

Cooking times may vary depending on the size of the lobster tails. Adjust the grilling time accordingly to ensure that the meat is fully cooked.

INSTRUCTIONS

1. Preheat the grill to medium-high heat.

2. Carefully cut the top shell of each lobster tail, keeping the meat intact and attached at the tail.

3. In a small bowl, combine the melted butter, minced garlic, lemon juice, salt, and pepper. Mix well to create a buttery seasoning.

4. Brush the buttery seasoning generously over the exposed lobster meat, making sure to cover all areas.

5. Grill the lobster tails, shell side down, with the lid closed, for 8-10 minutes until the meat is opaque, firm, and the shells are bright red. Baste with the remaining buttery seasoning while cooking.

6. Carefully remove the lobster tails from the grill and transfer them to a serving platter.

7. Garnish with fresh chopped parsley for added freshness and presentation.

8. Serve the grilled lobster tails immediately while hot, accompanied by melted butter or your favorite seafood dipping sauce.

CHAPTER 5

VEGETABLES AND SIDES

CAJUN BUTTERED CORN ON THE COB

Prep Time: 10 minutes | Cook Time: 15 minutes | Serving Size: 4

INGREDIENTS

- 4 ears of corn, husked
- 4 tablespoons unsalted butter, softened
- 1 teaspoon Cajun seasoning
- 1/2 teaspoon paprika
- 1/4 teaspoon garlic powder
- Salt, to taste
- Fresh parsley, chopped

 Adjust the amount of Cajun seasoning according to your desired level of spiciness. You can also customize the seasonings by adding other herbs and spices such as cayenne pepper, thyme, or onion powder.

INSTRUCTIONS

1. Preheat the grill to medium-high heat.
2. In a small bowl, mix together the softened butter, Cajun seasoning, paprika, garlic powder, and salt. Stir until well combined and the seasonings are evenly incorporated into the butter.
3. Brush each ear of corn generously with the Cajun butter mixture, making sure to coat all sides.
4. Place the corn directly on the grill grates and close the grill lid. Cook for about 12-15 minutes, turning occasionally, until the corn kernels are tender and lightly charred.
5. Remove the corn from the grill and transfer it to a serving platter.
6. Sprinkle with fresh chopped parsley for added freshness and color.
7. Serve the Cajun buttered corn on the cob hot and enjoy the flavorful and slightly spicy twist.

CINNAMON-SPICED SAUTEED APPLES

Prep Time: 10 minutes | Cook Time: 10 minutes | Serving Size: 4

INGREDIENTS

- 4 apples, peeled, cored, and sliced
- 2 tablespoons unsalted butter
- 2 tablespoons brown sugar
- 1 teaspoon ground cinnamon
- 1/4 teaspoon ground nutmeg
- 1/4 teaspoon vanilla extract

 You can adjust the amount of sugar and spices according to your taste preferences. Feel free to experiment with different types of apples for varying flavors and textures.

INSTRUCTIONS

1. Heat a large skillet or frying pan over medium heat.
2. Add the butter to the pan and let it melt until it starts to sizzle.
3. Add the sliced apples to the pan and spread them out in a single layer. Cook for about 5 minutes, stirring occasionally, until the apples begin to soften.
4. Sprinkle the brown sugar, ground cinnamon, and ground nutmeg (if using) over the apples. Stir well to coat the apples evenly with the spices and sugar.
5. Continue cooking the apples for another 5 minutes, or until they are tender and caramelized. Stir occasionally to prevent sticking and ensure even cooking.
6. If desired, add the vanilla extract to the pan and stir to incorporate it into the apples.
7. Remove the pan from the heat and let the sauteed apples cool slightly before serving.
8. Serve the cinnamon-spiced sauteed apples warm as a side dish or as a topping for pancakes, waffles, oatmeal, or ice cream.

SMOKED CORNBREAD POTLUCK SALAD

Prep Time: 20 minutes | Cook Time: 30 minutes | Serving Size: 8

INGREDIENTS

- 1 cup yellow cornmeal

- 1 cup all-purpose flour

- 1 tablespoon baking powder

- 1/2 teaspoon salt

- 1 cup buttermilk

- 1/4 cup vegetable oil

- 2 tablespoons honey

- 2 large eggs

Enjoy the smoky and flavorful combination of the smoked combread and fresh vegetables in this potluck salad!

INSTRUCTIONS

1. Preheat Traeger grill to 350°F (175°C) and preheat a cast-iron skillet.

2. Whisk together cornmeal, flour, baking powder, and salt in a bowl.

3. In a separate bowl, combine buttermilk, vegetable oil, honey, and eggs. Add wet ingredients to dry ingredients and mix.

4. Pour batter into the preheated skillet and place it on the grill. Smoke for 30 minutes until golden brown.

5. Let the smoked cornbread cool, then cut it into cubes.

6. Toss mixed salad greens, cherry tomatoes, corn kernels, diced red bell pepper, diced red onion, and cilantro in a large bowl.

7. Add smoked cornbread cubes to the salad mixture and toss gently.

8. Drizzle ranch dressing over the salad and toss to coat. Sprinkle with crumbled feta cheese if desired.

9. Serve immediately or refrigerate until ready to serve.

SEASONED SWEET POTATO WEDGES WITH DIPPING SAUCE

Prep Time: 15 minutes | Cook Time: 25 minutes | Serving Size: 4

INGREDIENTS

- 2 large sweet potatoes

- 2 tablespoons olive oil

- 1 teaspoon paprika

- 1/2 teaspoon garlic powder

- 1/2 teaspoon onion powder

- 1/2 teaspoon salt

- 1/4 teaspoon black pepper

Enjoy the crispy and flavorful seasoned sweet potato wedges with the tangy and creamy dipping sauce for a delicious snack or side dish!

INSTRUCTIONS

1. Preheat Traeger grill to 400°F (200°C).

2. Cut sweet potatoes into wedges, about 1/2-inch thick.

3. Combine olive oil, paprika, garlic powder, onion powder, salt, and black pepper in a bowl.

4. Toss sweet potato wedges in the seasoning mixture to coat evenly.

5. Arrange wedges on grill tray or grates in a single layer.

6. Grill for 20-25 minutes, flipping halfway, until tender and crispy.

7. Prepare dipping sauce: whisk mayo, ketchup, mustard, honey, vinegar, paprika, and cayenne (optional).

8. Remove wedges from grill and let them cool slightly.

9. Serve with dipping sauce on the side. Enjoy!

GARLIC PULL-APART BREAD

Prep Time: 10 minutes I Cook Time: 20 minutes I Serving Size: 4

INGREDIENTS

- 1 loaf of Italian bread or French bread
- 1/2 cup unsalted butter, melted
- 4 cloves of garlic, minced
- 2 tablespoons fresh parsley, chopped
- 1/2 teaspoon salt
- 1/4 teaspoon black pepper

INSTRUCTIONS

1. Preheat your Traeger grill to 375°F (190°C).
2. Using a serrated knife, make diagonal cuts across the loaf of bread, about 1 inch apart. Make sure not to cut all the way through the bottom of the bread, so that the loaf remains intact.
3. In a small bowl, combine the melted butter, minced garlic, chopped parsley, salt, and black pepper. Mix well to create the garlic butter mixture.
4. Brush the garlic butter mixture generously over the entire surface of the bread, making sure to get the mixture into the cuts.
5. Wrap the bread in aluminum foil, leaving the top exposed. Place the foil-wrapped bread on the preheated grill.
6. Close the lid of the grill and bake the bread for approximately 15-20 minutes, or until the bread is heated through and the butter has melted and infused with the garlic flavor.
7. Remove the foil-wrapped bread from the grill and carefully unwrap it.
8. Serve the garlic pull-apart bread warm. To enjoy, simply pull apart the individual sections of the bread, savoring the aromatic garlic and butter flavors.

SMOKED TWICE-BAKED POTATOES

Prep Time: 15 minutes I Cook Time: 2 hours I Serving Size: 4

INGREDIENTS

- 4 large baking potatoes
- 4 tablespoons unsalted butter, softened
- 1/2 cup sour cream
- 1/2 cup shredded cheddar cheese
- 4 slices bacon, cooked and crumbled
- 2 green onions, thinly sliced
- Salt and pepper to taste
- Wood chips or chunks for smoking

INSTRUCTIONS

1. Preheat Traeger grill to 350°F (175°C).
2. Wash and dry potatoes. Pierce them with a fork.
3. Smoke potatoes on grill for 1-2 hours until tender.
4. Remove potatoes and let them cool slightly.
5. Cut off top third of each potato and scoop out flesh.
6. Mix potato flesh with butter, sour cream, cheese, bacon, and green onions.
7. Spoon mixture back into potato shells.
8. Bake stuffed potatoes on grill for 15-20 minutes until cheese melts.
9. Let potatoes cool briefly before serving.
10. Enjoy smoked twice-baked potatoes as a side dish or main course. Garnish as desired.

BROCCOLI-CAULIFLOWER SALAD WITH CREAMY DRESSING

Prep Time: 15 minutes I Chill Time: 1 hour I Serving Size: 6

INGREDIENTS

For the Salad:

- 2 cups broccoli florets

- 2 cups cauliflower florets

- 1/2 cup chopped red onion

- 1/2 cup raisins

- 1/2 cup sliced almonds

For the Creamy Dressing:

- 1/2 cup mayonnaise

- 1/4 cup sour cream

- 2 tablespoons apple cider vinegar

- 2 tablespoons honey

- 1/2 teaspoon salt

- 1/4 teaspoon black pepper

INSTRUCTIONS

1. In a large bowl, combine the broccoli florets, cauliflower florets, chopped red onion, raisins, and sliced almonds. Toss to mix well.

2. In a separate bowl, whisk together the mayonnaise, sour cream, apple cider vinegar, honey, salt, and black pepper until smooth and creamy.

3. Pour the creamy dressing over the broccoli-cauliflower mixture. Use a spatula or spoon to gently toss and coat the vegetables with the dressing.

4. Cover the bowl with plastic wrap and refrigerate for at least 1 hour to allow the flavors to meld and the vegetables to soften slightly.

5. Once chilled, give the salad a final toss and adjust the seasoning if needed.

6. Serve the Broccoli-Cauliflower Salad chilled as a refreshing side dish or light lunch. It pairs well with grilled meats or can be enjoyed on its own.

BACON-WRAPPED GREEN BEANS

Prep Time: 15 minutes I Cook Time: 20 minutes I Serving Size: 4

INGREDIENTS

- 1 pound fresh green beans, ends trimmed

- 8 slices bacon

- 2 tablespoons olive oil

- 1/2 teaspoon garlic powder

- 1/2 teaspoon salt

- 1/4 teaspoon black pepper

INSTRUCTIONS

1. Preheat your Traeger grill to 375°F (190°C).

2. In a large bowl, toss the green beans with olive oil, garlic powder, salt, and black pepper until they are evenly coated.

3. Take a bundle of about 8-10 green beans and wrap a slice of bacon around the center, securing it with a toothpick. Repeat with the remaining green beans and bacon slices.

4. Place the bacon-wrapped green bean bundles directly on the grill grate.

5. Close the grill lid and cook for about 20 minutes, or until the bacon is crispy and the green beans are tender. You can also rotate the bundles halfway through cooking for even browning.

6. Carefully remove the bacon-wrapped green beans from the grill and transfer them to a serving platter.

7. Let them cool slightly before serving to avoid burns from the hot bacon.

CARAMELIZED BALSAMIC ONIONS WITH A TOUCH OF SWEETNESS

Prep Time: 15 minutes | Cook Time: 1 hour | Serving Size: 4

INGREDIENTS

- 4 large onions, thinly sliced
- 2 tablespoons olive oil
- 2 tablespoons butter
- 2 tablespoons brown sugar
- 1/4 cup balsamic vinegar
- 1/2 teaspoon salt
- 1/4 teaspoon black pepper

INSTRUCTIONS

1. Preheat Traeger grill to 400°F (200°C).
2. Thinly slice onions.
3. Place cast iron skillet or foil tray on grill grates.
4. Heat skillet for 5 minutes.
5. Add olive oil and butter to hot skillet.
6. Add sliced onions and spread evenly.
7. Sauté onions for 15-20 minutes, stirring occasionally.
8. Sprinkle brown sugar and drizzle balsamic vinegar over onions.
9. Lower heat to 350°F (175°C) and continue cooking for 30-40 minutes, stirring occasionally.
10. Season with salt and pepper.
11. Remove from grill.
12. Serve caramelized balsamic onions as a topping or accompaniment.

LOADED POTATO ROUNDS WITH TOPPINGS GALORE

Prep Time: 15 minutes | Cook Time: 30 minutes | Serving Size: 4

INGREDIENTS

- 4 large russet potatoes
- 2 tablespoons olive oil
- 1 teaspoon garlic powder
- 1 teaspoon paprika
- 1/2 teaspoon salt
- 1/4 teaspoon black pepper
- Toppings:
- Shredded cheddar cheese
- Cooked and crumbled bacon
- Chopped green onions
- Sour cream
- Salsa
- Guacamole
- Diced tomatoes
- Chopped cilantro

INSTRUCTIONS

1. Preheat oven to 425°F (220°C) and line a baking sheet.
2. Slice potatoes into rounds.
3. Toss potatoes with olive oil, garlic powder, paprika, salt, and pepper.
4. Arrange potatoes on baking sheet in a single layer.
5. Bake for 25-30 minutes until golden and crispy, flipping halfway.
6. Prepare desired toppings (cheese, bacon, onions, tomatoes, cilantro).
7. Remove potatoes from oven and let cool.
8. Load potatoes with toppings.
9. Serve as an appetizer or side dish.
10. Enjoy the loaded potato rounds with your favorite toppings.

SMOKY MAC AND CHEESE

Prep Time: 15 minutes | Cook Time: 1 hour | Serving Size: 6

INGREDIENTS

- 8 ounces elbow macaroni
- 2 tablespoons butter
- 2 tablespoons all-purpose flour
- 2 cups milk
- 2 cups shredded cheddar cheese
- 1 cup shredded smoked Gouda cheese
- 1 teaspoon smoked paprika
- 1/2 teaspoon garlic powder
- 1/2 teaspoon salt
- 1/4 teaspoon black pepper
- 1/4 teaspoon cayenne pepper
- 1/2 cup Panko breadcrumbs
- 2 tablespoons chopped fresh parsley

INSTRUCTIONS

1. Preheat Traeger grill to 375°F (190°C).
2. Cook macaroni until al dente, then drain.
3. Make cheese sauce on stovetop with butter, flour, milk, and seasonings.
4. Combine cooked macaroni with cheese sauce.
5. Transfer mixture to greased baking dish.
6. Place baking dish on Traeger grill.
7. Bake for 30-40 minutes until golden and bubbly.
8. Top with breadcrumbs.
9. Continue cooking for 10-15 minutes until breadcrumbs are golden brown.
10. Garnish with fresh parsley.
11. Serve hot as a main dish or side.

CAROLINA-STYLE BAKED BEANS WITH BBQ FLAVORS

Prep Time: 15 minutes | Cook Time: 2 hours | Serving Size: 6

INGREDIENTS

- 2 cans navy beans or Great Northern
  beans, drained and rinsed
- 1/2 cup barbecue sauce
- 1/4 cup ketchup
- 2 tablespoons yellow mustard
- 2 tablespoons apple cider vinegar
- 2 tablespoons brown sugar
- 1 tablespoon Worcestershire sauce
- 1/2 teaspoon garlic powder
- 1/2 teaspoon onion powder
- 1/4 teaspoon cayenne pepper
- 4 slices bacon, cooked and crumbled
- 1/2 cup diced onion
- Salt and black pepper to taste

INSTRUCTIONS

1. Preheat Traeger grill to 325°F (165°C).
2. Cook bacon until crispy, then crumble it.
3. Prepare sauce with barbecue sauce, ketchup, mustard, vinegar, sugar, Worcestershire, spices, and onion.
4. Add beans to sauce and stir to coat.
5. Place saucepan or Dutch oven on Traeger grill.
6. Cook for 1.5-2 hours, stirring occasionally.
7. Top with crumbled bacon.
8. Continue cooking for 10-15 minutes until bacon is crispy.
9. Serve as a side dish with BBQ meats or grilled burgers.

BLT PASTA SALAD WITH CREAMY DRESSING

Prep Time: 20 minutes I Cook Time: 10 minutes I Chill Time: 1 hour I Serving Size: 4-6

INGREDIENTS

For the Salad:

- 8 ounces rotini pasta

- 8 slices bacon, cooked and crumbled

- 2 cups cherry tomatoes, halved

- 2 cups lettuce, chopped

- 1/4 cup red onion, thinly sliced

- Salt and black pepper to taste

For the Creamy Dressing:

- 1/2 cup mayonnaise

- 1/4 cup sour cream

- 2 tablespoons fresh lemon juice

- 1 tablespoon Dijon mustard

- 1 clove garlic, minced

- 1/2 teaspoon sugar

- Salt and black pepper to taste

INSTRUCTIONS

1. Cook pasta until al dente, then drain and rinse with cold water.

2. Whisk together mayo, sour cream, lemon juice, mustard, garlic, sugar, salt, and pepper for the dressing.

3. Combine pasta, bacon, tomatoes, lettuce, and onion in a serving bowl.

4. Pour dressing over the salad and toss to coat.

5. Refrigerate for at least 1 hour to chill and allow flavors to meld.

6. Optional: Add avocado, feta cheese, or basil for extra flavor.

7. Serve chilled as a side dish or main course.

 If you prefer a vegetarian version, you can omit the bacon or replace it with vegetarian bacon alternatives. Customize the salad by adding other vegetables or herbs of your choice. Enjoy the refreshing and creamy flavors of the BLT Pasta Salad!

SPICY JALAPENO–CHEDDAR CORNBREAD

Prep Time: 15 minutes I Cook Time: 25-30 minutes I I Serving Size: 8

INGREDIENTS

- 1 cup cornmeal

- 1 cup all-purpose flour

- 1 tablespoon baking powder

- 1/2 teaspoon baking soda

- 1/2 teaspoon salt

- 1 cup buttermilk

- 2 large eggs

- 1/4 cup unsalted butter, melted

- 1 cup shredded cheddar cheese

- 2 jalapeno peppers, seeded and finely chopped

- 1/4 cup canned corn kernels, drained

- 1 tablespoon honey

INSTRUCTIONS

1. Preheat oven to 375°F (190°C). Grease a 9-inch square baking pan or cast iron skillet.

2. Mix dry ingredients: Combine cornmeal, flour, baking powder, baking soda, and salt in a bowl.

3. Prepare wet ingredients: Whisk buttermilk, eggs, and melted butter in a separate bowl.

4. Combine wet and dry ingredients: Pour wet mixture into the dry ingredients and stir until just combined.

5. Add jalapenos, cheese, and corn: Fold in chopped jalapenos, shredded cheddar cheese, and canned corn kernels.

6. Pour batter into pan: Transfer batter to greased pan, spreading it evenly.

7. Bake in the oven: Bake for 25-30 minutes until golden brown and a toothpick comes out clean.

8. Cool and serve: Let cool for a few minutes, then cut into squares or wedges. Serve warm.

9. Optional: Drizzle honey on top before serving for added sweetness.

SMOKY HOMEMADE SALSA WITH FRESH INGREDIENTS

Prep Time: 15 minutes I Cook Time: 10 minutes I Serving Size: 2

INGREDIENTS

- 4 medium tomatoes, diced
- 1 small red onion, finely chopped
- 2 jalapeno peppers, seeded and finely chopped
- 2 cloves garlic, minced
- 1/4 cup fresh cilantro, chopped
- Juice of 1 lime
- 1 tablespoon olive oil
- 1 teaspoon ground cumin
- 1/2 teaspoon smoked paprika
- Salt and black pepper to taste

 QUICK TIPS If you prefer a milder salsa, you can remove the seeds and membranes from the jalapeno peppers before chopping them.

INSTRUCTIONS

1. Prep the ingredients: Begin by dicing the tomatoes, finely chopping the red onion and jalapeno peppers, mincing the garlic, and chopping the fresh cilantro. Place them all into a mixing bowl.
2. Mix in the seasonings: Add the lime juice, olive oil, ground cumin, smoked paprika, salt, and black pepper to the bowl with the diced vegetables. If desired, you can also add chipotle powder for extra smokiness and sugar for a touch of sweetness.
3. Combine the ingredients: Gently stir all the ingredients together using a spoon or spatula, ensuring that the seasonings are evenly distributed and coating the vegetables.
4. Adjust the seasoning: Taste the salsa and adjust the salt, black pepper, and other seasonings according to your preference. You can add more lime juice for extra tang or more jalapeno peppers for additional heat.
5. Let the flavors meld: Cover the bowl with plastic wrap or a lid and refrigerate for at least 1 hour, allowing the flavors to meld together and develop.
6. Serve the smoky homemade salsa chilled and enjoy it with tortilla chips or as a flavorful topping for various dishes like tacos, nachos, or grilled meats.

SPICY JALAPENO-CHEDDAR CORNBREAD

Prep Time: 15 minutes I Cook Time: 25-30 minutes I I Serving Size: 8

INGREDIENTS

- 1 cup cornmeal
- 1 cup all-purpose flour
- 1 tablespoon baking powder
- 1/2 teaspoon baking soda
- 1/2 teaspoon salt
- 1 cup buttermilk
- 2 large eggs
- 1/4 cup unsalted butter, melted
- 1 cup shredded cheddar cheese
- 2 jalapeno peppers, seeded and finely chopped
- 1/4 cup canned corn kernels, drained
- 1 tablespoon honey

INSTRUCTIONS

1. Preheat oven to 375°F (190°C). Grease a 9-inch square baking pan or cast iron skillet.
2. Mix dry ingredients: Combine cornmeal, flour, baking powder, baking soda, and salt in a bowl.
3. Prepare wet ingredients: Whisk buttermilk, eggs, and melted butter in a separate bowl.
4. Combine wet and dry ingredients: Pour wet mixture into the dry ingredients and stir until just combined.
5. Add jalapenos, cheese, and corn: Fold in chopped jalapenos, shredded cheddar cheese, and canned corn kernels.
6. Pour batter into pan: Transfer batter to greased pan, spreading it evenly.
7. Bake in the oven: Bake for 25-30 minutes until golden brown and a toothpick comes out clean.
8. Cool and serve: Let cool for a few minutes, then cut into squares or wedges. Serve warm.
9. Optional: Drizzle honey on top before serving for added sweetness.

APPENDIX: MEASUREMENT CON-VERSION CHART

MEASUREMENT CONVERSION CHART

VOLUME EQUIVALENTS(DRY)

US STANDARD	METRIC (APPROXIMATE)
1/8 teaspoon	0.5 mL
1/4 teaspoon	1 mL
1/2 teaspoon	2 mL
3/4 teaspoon	4 mL
1 teaspoon	5 mL
1 tablespoon	15 mL
1/4 cup	59 mL
1/2 cup	118 mL
3/4 cup	177 mL
1 cup	235 mL
2 cups	475 mL
3 cups	700 mL
4 cups	1L

VOLUME EQUIVALENTS(LIQUID)

US STANDARD	US STANDARD (US STANDARD)	METRIC (APPROXIMATE)
2 tablespoons	1 fl.oz.	30 mL
1/4 cup	2 fl.oz.	60 mL
1/2 cup	4 fl.oz.	120 mL
1 cup	8 fl.oz.	240 mL
1 1/2 cup	12 fl.oz.	355 mL
2 cups or 1 pint	16 fl.oz.	475 mL
4 cups or 1 quart	32 fl.oz.	1 L
1 gallon	128 fl.oz.	4 L

TEMPERATURES EQUIVALENTS

FAHRENHEIT(F)	CELSIUS(C)
225 °F	107 °C
250 °F	120 °C
275 °F	135 °C
300 °F	150 °C
325 °F	160 °C
350 °F	180 °C
375 °F	190 °C
400 °F	205 °C
425 °F	220 °C
450 °F	235 °C
475 °F	245 °C
500 °F	260°C

WEIGHT EQUIVALENTS

US STANDARD	METRIC (APPROXIMATE)
1 ounce	28 g
2 ounces	57 g
5 ounces	142 g
10 ounces	284 g
15 ounces	425 g
16 ounces	455 g
1.5 pounds	680 g
2 pounds	907 g

Made in the USA
Las Vegas, NV
05 February 2024

85324853R00046